SAWDUSTED

Terrace Books, a trade imprint of the University of Wisconsin Press,
takes its name from the Memorial Union Terrace, located at
the University of Wisconsin–Madison. Since its inception in 1907,
the Wisconsin Union has provided a venue for students, faculty, staff,
and alumni to debate art, music, politics, and the issues of the day.
It is a place where theater, music, drama, literature, dance, outdoor activities,
and major speakers are made available to the campus and the community.
To learn more about the Union, visit www.union.wisc.edu.

SAWDUSTED

NOTES FROM
A POST-BOOM MILL

RAYMOND GOODWIN

TERRACE BOOKS
A TRADE IMPRINT OF THE UNIVERSITY OF WISCONSIN PRESS

Terrace Books
A trade imprint of the University of Wisconsin Press
1930 Monroe Street, 3rd Floor
Madison, Wisconsin 53711-2059
uwpress.wisc.edu

3 Henrietta Street
London WCE 8LU, England
eurospanbookstore.com

1   3   5   4   2

Printed in the United States of America

Library of Congress Cataloging-in-Publication Data
Goodwin, Raymond, 1959–
Sawdusted: notes from a post-boom mill / Raymond Goodwin.
        p.   cm.
ISBN 978-0-299-23570-3 (cloth: alk. paper)
ISBN 978-0-299-23573-4 (e-book)
    1. Goodwin, Raymond, 1959–
2. Sawmill workers—Michigan—Biography.   I. Title.
HD8039.S32.U6G66   2010
    674'.2092—dc22
        [B]
    2009041309

While most names have been changed, all persons described in the following pages are real.
There are no composite characters or invented circumstances.

For
DEBBIE
ROGER
PETER

And in loving memory of
RANDY J. GOODWIN

CONTENTS

SAWDUSTED

MUSEUMS

O N A LEAFY SATURDAY in October of 1993, in a
local hub called Whipple's, I paid for my burger and
fries, sat down at a table with a red-and-white checkered
tablecloth, and began to eat. Back in the corner snack bar, I
was the lone customer. As I slurped my Coca-Cola, I mar-
veled at the setting: Moorestown, Michigan, was home to
fifty denim and flannel souls, a Methodist church, a township hall, and, immediately, the remarkable Whipple's. Here,
under one roof, was a gas station, a repair shop, a liquor
shelf, two aisles of groceries, a clothing rack, a bakery, and
the eatery. To exaggerate only slightly, in twenty steps you
could fill your basket with a loaf of bread, a fan belt, a five-
pound ham, a fifth of whiskey, a pair of finely woven hunting socks, and enough licorice to harness a team of oxen. In
another ten steps, you could fill your bicycle tire with air and
your pickup with premium. With the shopping done, you
could lean back and enjoy a slice of pizza or a wedge of apple
pie. Whipple's, in short, was the town's entire economy.

Sitting in my metal folding chair, I thought all the building lacked was its own zip code. Cluttered but contained, its
compression was soothing somehow; an entire world, rural

and no nonsense, was within arm's reach. With the carpet absorbing the hubbub at the front of the store, it was so quiet I began to relax. I had driven out to the old logging country to savor the landscape, to molt the tension from my neck, to breathe easily again, and Whipple's was perfect.

Most of the fries and half the burger were down before I noticed that this corner was more than just a snack bar; it was also a minimuseum of Moorestown history. There were no theater ropes or fancy lighting, and no doubt the curator and the cook were one and the same person, but it was a museum nonetheless, the exhibits neat and unpretentious. Mounted on the wall above me were a large crosscut saw, a bucksaw, and a scatter of log markers. Strung from the ceiling, like a rusty quarter moon with a handle, was a scythe. Dangling nearby were various hooks, grippers, and pliers— rustic tools from yesteryear—and on the back wall a tiny school of wooden fish swam north. There were photographs, too, lower on the wall, at eye level from the chair, a dozen black and whites in sturdy frames. It was these photographs, a hundred years old if they were a day, that pulled my attention from the burger and put a wrinkle in my contentment.

One was of a general store that no longer existed; another was of two men, teamsters, posing with their horses and wagon; and a third was a portrait of the town's founder, a white-bearded man named J. Henry Moores. Another, smaller photograph, jammed into the corner of a large frame, was of a party of men hoisting steins of beer in a hotel bar. Yet another—and here my chewing slowed—was of twenty or so men gathered in front of the sun-drenched wall of a sawmill.

Gazing at this last photograph, I felt my chest puff a mighty two inches. I was worthy. A former sawmill worker myself, I had been part of the great Michigan lumbering tradition, albeit three generations removed from its glory days. I had stacked lumber, the grunt work. At a mill in nearby Lake City, the county seat, I had worked with thirty men as hardy as those looking back from the photograph. In a long, boisterous building on the east end of town, we had measured, cut, and stacked thousands of board feet of oak, pine, and popple, wood that would ultimately become pallets, furniture, and railroad ties. We had worked in grueling heat, arctic cold, snow, sleet, haze, and hail, pulling muscles, breaking bones, and twisting joints as if they were as flimsy as burlap. We were worthy, indeed.

Yet something inside me wouldn't settle. I stared at the wall for several more minutes before it hit me, you might say, like a flying cord of firewood. I realized that those men in the frames had willingly stood to be photographed. They were from the heyday of Michigan's lumbering era, the time of lumberjacks, river drives, horse-drawn wagons loaded down with logs, and pine trees reaching for the sky; they were figures of legend and lore, and you could see in their posture, in their readiness to pose, that they were proud of their place in the sawdust and in history.

Contrarily, had a photographer set up at the sawmill I had worked in, most of the crew would have laughed in scorn or run from his shutter. By the time I began stacking planks for a living in the early winter of 1979, the heyday was long over. Nostalgia aside, I remembered the mill as a place of hard work and low pay, a place of slivers and blood, a place you had arrived at out of desperation for any job to help pay the rent. A photograph of our defeated mugs would have been proof of our failure to find respectable work. It was hardly a legacy to hang on a wall.

Of course I was wrong, and the men in the photograph knew it; moreover, as I pushed aside my lunch, I knew what they were thinking. When the dead look back at you with their glaring, imploring eyes, the one, the *only* thing on their minds is that you remember them. Those men against the sawmill wall were telling me that their presence on the planet, as trifling as it might be judged, was an example to those who would come after them. While it was true the example was up for smear and ridicule, it was no less true that it was up for emulation and admiration.

Their gaze was telling me that it was my turn to make an offering, a link to the future, as they had done by standing for the photograph. My argument—that the sawmill in my day was a wilted pine, a place scraping the bottom of the economy instead of its new golden chip (as it had been in their day), a place in which no one would be interested—was no argument. That I didn't have a camera and actual bodies to photograph was no excuse either. I had something just as good, they said, for wasn't my mind already trundling back through the years to the sawmill? Wasn't I already seeing the faces and hearing the voices of the men I had worked with as if they were standing next to me? I had memory. I had a mountain of memories. I remembered the mill as if I'd just stepped though its big sliding door: a battered aluminum barn that always reminded me of a Great Lakes freighter run aground. It was seventy yards long and twenty-five yards wide and looked sturdy enough to haul a load of iron ore from Duluth to Detroit and back. Nearby was a smaller tugboat of a building (home to the office, break room, and saw-filing room), a range of snowcapped sawdust mountains, and huddled rows of pallets and cants that resembled a rickety city skyline. I could even recall the ground over which the crew had trod, a mix of sand, clay, sawdust, wood chips, and pulverized bark crisscrossed with forklift tracks deep enough to tear ligaments in. It was a harsh, gray setting, and my opinion had always been that it was the most forsaken three acres I had ever seen.

But did it have to be forsaken? Sitting at the checkered table, I wondered if it was the men I had worked with and our attitude toward the mill that had rendered it so. I could easily conjure Whiskey-Tim and Lanny Boy, the Cat, the Rat, the Rookie, and the Tattoo Man as plainly as I was seeing those men in the photograph. In the same snapshot of memory were Dar-Dar, the Animal, and Blanched Duane. Big Tom and the Good Ole Boys were there, as was Lightning Joe, and in the center of it all was my older brother, Randy. Randy with his arms crossed, almost smiling. Were we the forsakers?

It was an unsettling thought, but the men in the photograph were telling me it wasn't too late to clean up my attitude. More to the point, they were telling me there was really no choice; to be a forsaker was to be forgotten. Their gaze was dire yet somehow patient, but I knew their patience wouldn't last forever. So I stood and made a silent promise to

keep our extended history, our common ground, from erod-
ing from memory like sawdust blown off the roof of a windswept mill. The words of this essay are the beginning of that
attempt.

As I threaded my way out of Whipple's that autumn day,
I was guilt stricken and less content but feeling better. For
the first time I understood that there was a museum in my
head.

AUTHORIZATION

IT WAS POSTED on a small, square sign on the fence: AUTHORIZED PERSONNEL ONLY.

As I followed Randy through the gate on my first morning at the sawmill, I couldn't help asking, "Who are authorized personnel?"

Randy hunched his shoulders against the cold and pondered the question. A two-time college dropout, I was twenty years old and more adept at asking questions than developing answers for them. I had recently come home from Lansing, where I'd worked for a railroad demolition company that had gone bankrupt. My homecoming plan was to find work in a grocery store or even a gas station, but Randy had reminded me that working in a store meant wearing a tie (read noose) and that both a store and a station meant working with the public. The public, he said, could be gruesome. Actually, what he said was that the public was the largest SOB in existence. Behind the barbed-wire fence of the sawmill, he told me without a whit of irony, I would be safe from the public.

As we crossed the mill yard, he pulled so hard on his cigarette that his cheeks hollowed. After what seemed a full minute, he blew out the smoke and pitched the smolder into a snowdrift.

"Authorized personnel?" he said, shaking his head. "Anyone who can walk." And then he laughed into the dawn.

My notion of a sawmill manager was of a thin, garrulous old man with a greasy cap skewed on his gray, mottled head, but the manager I worked for beginning in the early winter of 1979 didn't come within a mile of this description. He was thirty years old, as gruff and brooding as a grizzly bear, and with shoulders so wide they stretched the seams of his canvas jacket. His hard hat, tipped at a sly angle, was covered with a thousand tiny scratches as if it had been flung repeatedly and with relish across a corrugated concrete floor. The manager had a broad, intelligent forehead and eyes bright if somewhat sullen. He seemed always wounded to me, although I was never able to identify the thorn's point of entry.

All these years later it occurs to me that he might have been self-conscious about his voice, for it was a deep voice, a voice purged from gravel. So deep was this voice that you figured there was a good yard between the roof of his mouth and his larynx. Randy had given me tips for the interview that first morning—be sure to mention that I'd worked in a sawmill before, forget that my last job had lasted only six weeks—but about this voice he'd said nothing. Worse, after hurried introductions in the dingy office, he'd gone out, leaving me alone with the manager. This, I want you to know, is properly called abandonment.

Standing before the manager's big desk, I felt like some poor seventeenth-century English trapper hauled out of the Quebec woods to face the French magistrate without a translator. I didn't know which of us to feel sorrier for. The manager would churn his gravel with a question—I could tell it was a question by the tone—and I'd ask him to repeat it once, twice, a third time, all to no avail. When your ears expect sawdust but get stones instead, things turn desperate in a hurry.

I was thinking I should sneak out and sell pencils for a living when I thought I heard him utter Randy's name. I blurted a "Yes!" so loudly that the corners of his mouth turned up, not quite a grin but encouraging. He then parted the heaps of lumber receipts on his desk, found an application for employment and a pen wide enough to bolt a barn door with, shoved both at me, and pointed to a large wooden chair with an arm desk. I peddled back two steps and sat down, in school again, as it were.

As I filled the spaces on the application (the smallest writing spaces in the world are reserved for employment applications), the manager marched out to throw power switches in the sawmill. With the noise of revving machinery, the ground shook and the office windows vibrated, though for all I knew this was caused by the footsteps of this lumbering, latter-day Paul Bunyan. When he returned, he stomped the snow from his boots with enough force to topple redwoods, snatched the application from my hand, and began to scan it. A moment later he looked up and called me "Uriah." It sounded biblical, but, knowing I was no kind of prophet, I

translated this as "You're hired," an accurate rendering. I suspected Randy had pulled some strings and possibly laid
down an ultimatum of the "Hire my kid brother or else"
variety, and the manager, knowing good sawyers were hard
to come by, had relented.

But as I stood and we shook hands, I knew high drama
had played no part in it. I recalled an exchange at my first
sawmill, an old shack of a place over in Roscommon County,
where I'd worked for six weeks (courtesy, again, of Randy's
influence) after graduating from high school. There, during
break time one morning, one of the more opinionated hands
told the owner that if he would pay a better wage the turn-
over rate among his employees would be lower. The owner, a
squat man with an orange rag hanging perpetually from his
hip pocket, rolled his yellow eyes as if it were the most ludi-
crous thing he'd ever heard. "Hell," he said, dismissing the
notion, "I've run half the county through here and still have
the other half to go." At this new mill it was no different. My
hiring, as well as my nearly nonexistent relationship with
management over the next twenty months, was no more
complicated than my being among the wrong half of the
county.

But hired I was, and the manager figured he'd better do
something with me. He rummaged his desk again, handed
me a medical evaluation form and the key to the company
pickup, and pointed over my head toward town. With an
iron set to his jaw, he graveled out two words that sounded
like "post office." Did he want me to pick up the mail while
I was out? No, that wasn't it; the doctor's office was across
the street from the post office. I was on my way to a physical

examination. I stepped back into the cold thinking I'd rather be taking a calculus test.

But as much as I despised visits to the doctor, and nothing crimped my day more, that wasn't the dread that consumed me. As I drove away, again passing the AUTHORIZED PERSONNEL ONLY sign, I was feeling a primordial ache. It was the ache of all new men to be free of the awkward, get-to-know-ya stuff and be truly authorized. But authorization—true "I'm in and can't be budged" authorization—was tricky. This exalted standing meant things like inquiries about your weekend, your deer stand, and your family life. It was referral to your opinion about work matters and respect for your Super Bowl pick. Your fellow mill hands had to silently bestow authorization on you, yet at the same time, silently, you had to declare it for yourself. Tricky.

At the doctor's office a grim-faced nurse led me down a dark hallway to the examination room. She pointed me up onto a padded table and told me the doctor would be along soon. Always edgy in medical environs, I was comforted by the old-fashioned eye chart on the wall, the Norman Rockwell print of the little fella with the unhitched britches checking out the doctor's diploma, and the quality of the morning light bleeding through the venetian blinds. It was so peaceful, had the table been a foot longer I might have stretched out and fallen asleep.

A few minutes later the doctor, a gaunt Asian man, entered. The examination lamp strapped to his forehead gave him the mien of an ornery miner from copper country. I waited for more gravel, but his voice, a veritable rose compared to the manager's stones, was gentle and calm. As he

washed his hands, I asked myself what the difference was
between those who pursued and obtained medical degrees
and others—like me, for instance—who seemed hell-bent
for bootfuls of sawdust and oblivion. I didn't come up with
an answer, but it made me glad that the doctor was the one
asking the questions. He dried his hands on a paper towel,
hugged a clipboard to his chest, and leaned toward me. Had
I ever had a serious illness?

"Hepatitis as a child," I said.

"Any illness, recently?"

"No."

"Do you smoke?"

"No."

"Allergies?"

"What?"

"Have you ever had any allergies?"

"None that I know of."

The doctor marked something on the clipboard and set
it aside. With measured strokes, he checked my heart rate,
my blood pressure, and, with a tiny ball-peen hammer, the
reflexes in my knees. He looked into my eyes with a small
flashlight and asked if I used drugs, and when I said no he
gave such a doglike tilt of the head that I wondered what the
usual answer to this question was.

"Well, you're strong as a horse," he said finally, and I slid
off the table, thinking the physical was over. But no. While
my back was turned, the doctor sidled up to a cabinet and
opened a drawer. He told me to drop my trousers, bend over,
and grab my ankles. It sounded like a stretching exercise the
coaches in high school used to demand, only then you kept

your gym shorts up. As I slid my hands down my shins, I felt nothing would ever be normal again. The blood rushed to my head, a bucketful. When I heard the crumpling of cellophane, I gave a passing thought to that mining lamp on his forehead and closed my eyes. A second later I heard the rubber glove snap on, and a second after that, because it was my decision to make, to hell with what anyone else thought, I was authorized.

A SHOT OF WHISKEY

IF STORIES FROM WOODSTOVE RACONTEURS of a hundred years ago are to be believed, the old forests grew zany characters almost as plentiful as trees. Scoundrels, murderers, thieves, and the terminally wayward all beat a path to the logjam. Peer into any of the old photographs and along with the pleas for remembrance you'll see the wild-eyed stares and sense the insanity, or the hilarity, or maybe both, about to metastasize once the camera was hooded and packed away.

My elfin friend Whiskey-Tim fit several of these categories, including that of the most cheerful man I'd ever met in my life. My first morning at the sawmill he rounded the green chains, strode directly up to me, and shook my hand. With more than a passing resemblance to the actor Danny DeVito (who, I learned later, he happened to think was the greatest actor of our time), he was stubby in trunk, neck, and limb, and when he grinned the gap between his front teeth was wide enough to wiggle a wood chip through. In his denim coveralls and overcoat, he might have been a third portrait in *American Gothic*, with that gloomy couple with the pitchfork, as the farmer's innocent son. Through the

roar of the saws, Tim uttered the six words all new men long
to hear. "I'll show you what to do," he said. He thereby se-
cured a permanent place in my affections.

Tim worked the green chains, considered the worst job
in the sawmill, and for nearly two years we would work
them side by side. The green chains, or "the chain," or sometimes "the chains," were just that, five flat, linked chains,
each in its own narrow track, two feet apart and three feet off
the floor (when I explained my job to those who had never
worked in a mill—civilians, we called them   I referred to
the green chains as simply the conveyor). The chains turned
on a common sprocket at three miles an hour and carried
the wood down from the roll cases of the head saws to the
stacking area.

I thought of the chains as the waterfront of the sawmill.
They were the dock on which the hard physical labor was
done, where the wood was stacked onto wooden runners
until there were twenty or thirty or even forty stacks neatly
built and banded for the daily load. (The wood was then
hauled to the north end of the mill to be turned into pallets,
transported to a sister mill near Lapeer, or sold to one of the
furniture companies in Grand Rapids.) The chains were
where the meatiest gossip was born, where more than anywhere else in the mill weariness turned more quickly to
complaint, and where vileness was most often confused with
virility. It was where the union talk began (someone would
always have an uncle who was an organizer) and where it
died out (someone would always point out the owner's

position, which was to board up the place and let it rot
rather than see it overrun by communists). The chains was
the job from which the man who had inquired about work
on Monday, was interviewed Tuesday, was hired on Wednes-
day, and worked his first day on Thursday quit on Friday. It
was where at times stacking one piece of wood on another
seemed almost a simple pleasure, where the click of wood on
wood could sound almost musical, but where, you learned,
building all those stacks would take its toll on you, that on
that little patch of concrete floor near the big sliding door
you would leave a part of yourself each day.

But if Whiskey-Tim was aware of any of this, he was too
busy to let on. That first morning he showed me the "technique" of stacking cants. A cant is a log that has been slabbed
off to make it more or less square. It is typically six to twelve
feet in length and weighs between one hundred and three
hundred pounds.

With his face clenched in determination, Tim pulled the
end of a long oak cant a foot over the edge of the chain,
turned a full one-eighty, threw his right arm over the top of
the cant, and gripped it as you might a rolled-up sleeping
bag. Then, guiding with his left hand and tugging with his
right, he took three bowlinglike steps forward, set the front
of the cant onto the stack, and with a thrust slid the whole
into place. Pull, turn, step, set, slide. It was a five-step sawmill dance, more timing and physics than brute strength.

My first try at the technique was a disaster. I thrust too
hard and sent the cant careening off the stack to the floor
with a thud so loud and solid it tickled my eardrums. While
the old men of the gang saw crew stared at me through the

rising dust cloud, Whiskey-Tim rushed around the stack and grabbed the far end of the cant, and together we set the thing into place.

"It won't take long before you get it," he said, soothing words amid the racket.

And he was right. By noon of that first day I had gone from apprentice to journeyman, and by week's end I was a master stacker. There were greater triumphs at the mill— avoiding broken bones, among them—but to heave and slide a cant firmly into place, to know it had been your toil that had formed the cants into a stack, to have molded individuals into a unit, why, there was something of the drill sergeant's thrill in it despite your bleeding hands.

Everywhere I turned that first week it seemed Whiskey-Tim was nearby, nodding his approval. For the first time in years, I felt like a prized student.

When I arrived at the sawmill that winter, Whiskey-Tim had been working the chain for six weeks, by far the longest tenure among the stackers. He claimed the hard work made his wind better, helped him to lose weight so his clothes fit looser, and allowed him a sounder sleep at night. This Boy Scout's view confirmed my first impression that Whiskey-Tim was as innocent as a cherub. He was so foursquare and pious about his work duties that I was sure these sentiments must extend to his nonmill life, too.

Tim lived at home with his mother, and I had no doubt that, at age twenty-three, he was not only his mother's boy but the very light in her life. It was easy to imagine him driving her to the supermarket, dropping her at church meetings, and spending quiet evenings with her, playing backgammon or clipping coupons from the newspaper. Imagining this, you could easily imagine him waking in the morning, pulling on freshly laundered work clothes, and breakfasting in the electric warmth of her kitchen. Then down Gladwin Street he'd go, sidestepping the sleds and tricycles left out by the neighborhood kids, walking the cracked sidewalks halfway across town until he rounded the corner onto Bacon Street, where Randy and I would see him as we waited in the truck for the work day to begin. I'll admit something inside me eased whenever Whiskey-Tim rounded that corner. We worked well together and it was a comfort knowing that not everyone at the sawmill was hard-bitten and gruff.

And as happy as I was with Whiskey, he seemed just as happy with me. His previous stacking partners had all gone sawmill AWOL for one reason or another, but now he couldn't keep the grin off his face. Along with demonstrating the technique, he showed me how to unclog the chipper and band a stack of cants and brought me Coca-Colas from the break room. When his turn came to stack the wood, he moved quickly, eager to prove he wasn't about to shift all the work onto the new man.

Had we been ratcheted back a hundred years to the days of pine and glory, Tim and I would have been a lumberjack team. We would have hauled our axes deep into the forest, chopped a notch into a big pine, and set to work with our crosscut saw, a man at each end, pulling back and forth until the tree was felled. Lumberjacking required much more teamwork than the popular image imparts, and Whiskey and I applied a similar ethic to stacking the boards and cants.

But as satisfying as conquering the heavy load was, the best part about working with Whiskey-Tim was the conversation. Sometimes it was about work or the weather but more often about baseball and boxing. Tim kept clippings in his wallet of the previous summer's American League batting leaders, and we'd spend hours discussing the hitters' stances and statistics. When the saws were down, we'd pitch chunks of wood to each other, swatting them through the big entrance with a board we'd pried from a pallet, dreaming we were in the friendly confines of Tiger Stadium or Fenway Park.

One day Tim brought in boxing magazines with vintage photographs of all the greats. On the flimsy pages were action shots of Joe Louis, Rocky Marciano, Muhammad Ali, and Smokin' Joe Frazier, and in the slim moments between work on the cants and boards we'd analyze boxing strategies, admiring the dance and rope-a-dope of Ali one minute, the attack and flail of Marvelous Marvin Hagler the next. Tim told me had he grown up in the era of the Friday Night Fights he would have lived his life planted on a bar stool in front of a TV in New York City, and in my mind's eye I conjured up a black-and-white photograph of this rotund little man doing just that.

It was marvelous: the fantasy, the clippings, the magazines, all of it. I felt my imaginary authorization card had been stamped with a big seal of approval. Then one morning in my second week at the mill, while I was in the throes of thinking what a good man this mother-loving homebody was, Tim turned to me after stacking a particularly heavy cant and said, "I haven't worked this hard since I was incarcerated in the Nevada State Penitentiary."

TIMBERRRR!!!!

Now, honestly, I wasn't entirely shocked. I'll admit my knees wobbled a bit, but I didn't go down. Although in those days I was a couple of cants shy of a full stack, even I knew a place like the sawmill wasn't likely to attract pure innocence. Besides, the brain is a funny dumpling, a haywire of wires, comparing, analyzing, and shuffling information into new slots, which is to say chances are it will adjust to dubious news. My very calm hope was that Tim's incarceration wasn't for a violent crime. As I had my back to him about half the time, violence would have meant a new set of parameters for our relationship.

"Yeah?" I said, gulped just the one time, and asked, "What kind of trouble were you in?"

Whiskey-Tim smiled. Not a smile of guile but his usual cheerful grin. "Grand Theft," he said with pride.

A weight fled my chest. Not murder. Not assault. Good enough. A confession of the felonious demanded space, so for the time being I decided not to pinch Tim for more information. Besides, for Tim to talk about his life hardly required prodding. Over the next few days he told me about growing up in rural Nevada, dreaming he'd one day find fortune in the silver mines around Battle Mountain or on the casino floor in Reno. He told me about his boyhood troubles with the school authorities ("Me and the principal didn't see eye to eye" was the crisp explanation), described his souring relationship with his mother and sister, and added other snippets of family history. The idyll I had imagined for his home life had never existed.

One morning, after he'd described his career as a shoplifter—a gig that had led to the grand theft charge—I saw my opening.

"So," I said, "what kind of car was it?"

"What car?"

"The grand theft."

"It wasn't a car," Whiskey-Tim said. "It was plumbing supplies."

Four thousand dollars worth when the loot was counted up. Tim had stolen copper tubing, putty knives, and assorted pipes and valves from the plumbing store he clerked in as revenge for a promised raise the owner had neglected to remit. He'd planned the heist to the smallest detail, from sneaking in the back door after hours to arranging the getaway car, but overlooked the most important detail: the back door's silent alarm. As he waited for his ride to pawnshop glory, it wasn't a getaway but a squad car that pulled up to greet him. At the thought of master criminal Whiskey-Tim standing in the alley among his commodes, I had to stifle a laugh. The judge didn't find it so funny, however, and when the gavel came down Whiskey-Tim had eighteen months in the pen.

Tim told me the worst thing about prison was the work details in the fields outside the walls, where the inmates picked potatoes. He hated picking those potatoes. I thought if picking potatoes was the worst of it in the Big House then he was luckier than he seemed to realize, but I didn't say it. In any case Whiskey-Tim had already made up his own mind about prison.

Overall, he thought it was just what he needed, although he couldn't claim to miss it much.

Whiskey-Tim's prison stories were surprisingly mundane, but his other tales of Nevada—those about cathouses, for instance—flooded my censures and washed modesty down the canyon. Tim claimed to have visited the "ranches" a good dozen times, and I found myself asking question after question, figuring as long as we were sealed off from eavesdroppers by the big noise in the sawmill I might as well hear a little about the larger world (besides, frothing saliva glands demand a catharsis). And Whiskey-Tim was happy to oblige. Between boards I got a firsthand account of ranching in the Wild West.

It seems it all started with a dating ritual as old as the silver-mining hills. The short version is you took your girl to dinner and a movie, and later, after a kiss goodnight (or good-bye, not necessarily the same thing), she dropped you at one of the ranches. True, you had to make your way home across the desert as best you could but with a grin wider than the Hoover Dam. This accommodation seemed beyond the tolerance of even the best-natured girlfriends I'd ever had, but Whiskey-Tim said it was a matter of course in Nevada that some ladies, duly wined and dined, preferred to take the rough carpenter's view and leave the finish work to the professionals. Most of us believe in the division of labor to one degree or another, but maybe this nudges the limits. Anyway, from entering the ranch house parlors—some of the plushest rooms he'd ever been in, with shag carpeting an inch thick, fancy suede unicorn paintings, velvet-covered chairs, and a wet bar along the wall—to the business upstairs, Tim described it all with patience and precision, as if explaining the relationship between plate tectonics and earthquakes.

When I asked about the girls, Whiskey-Tim flashed that gap-toothed grin. He said most were young women willing to toss aside virtue for the small fortune that could be made in a relatively short time; to them it was just a job, with no more emotion invested than it took to iron shirts in a laundry room. I wondered if this could really be the case, for wouldn't the time come when they would mourn that virtue like nothing they had ever mourned before? Even if only for a moment? I didn't pursue the point. Tim seemed to know a lot more about it than I did. He also said most of the girls were about our age and venereal disease wasn't a worry because the Nevada State Health Department made regular rounds to ensure that, as he put it, "the girls were clean." Sometimes when the wind was blowing off the sneer of a big blue and black, bellicose cloud over Norwich Township, wind with ice in it, I'd swallow my guilt and think about those warm, clean girls about our age and long for Nevada, home of the mountain bluebird. Then a board would slip from my grip and land on my toes, and—reality come callin'—I'd snap out of it, happy to be at home in Michigan and in just enough pain for that old adage to be a lesson: *Keep your mind on your work.*

One morning I explained to Tim that we could measure how hard we were working with a scientific formula I'd learned in college. Having dropped out so often, maybe I was nostalgic for the classroom, or, having become a lumber stacker in earnest, it was possible I was developing a craftsman's inclination to apply science to my trade. Whatever the case, I knew the explanation lacked the aplomb of Tim's ranch stories, but I kept going anyway.

"They're called foot-pounds," I told him, and recited the formula: weight times distance equals foot-pounds or the measurement of work. I took a nail and, in the dust of an old board, scratched out a calculation of the number of foot-pounds Tim and I accumulated by stacking a load of oak cants. The product, a figure over two million, made Whiskey blink.

After he'd turned it over in his mind a moment, he smiled, and as he shook his head, I knew we were thinking the same thing. All that work and we were barely paid the minimum wage; whorehouses weren't the only places where you got screwed.

During my last spring at the mill, Whiskey-Tim fell in love. The girl was fifteen years old, and her name was Cheri. We couldn't forget her name because Tim never stopped saying it. It was Cheri this, Cheri that, Cheri said, so you should, too. I'm pretty sure Tim believed Cheri had invented space travel.

They had stumbled into one another at a party. It was a relatively elegant affair, not too deep in the woods, the bonfire fueled by an old oak stump instead of the ripped-out seat of a Pontiac. Whiskey-Tim allowed Cheri to sip from his Budweiser and later bought her a pack of cigarettes. Cheri told him he was cool—a word of silk to soothe the rough-hewn breast—and that, doubtless, was the moment he fell for her. Not even the girls back at the ranch had told him that.

But it was destitute love from the beginning. Red Eye, a sawyer at the mill who often partied with Whiskey, told us the girl used poor Tim to buy her alcohol and cigarettes and was then lean with the rewards. Gossip in a sawmill is just more slivers and spit, but when word got around that all Whiskey had received for his devotion was a few tepid kisses, many of the crew found it hard to look him in the eye with a straight face.

And he talked about her. That was bad enough, but he talked about her talking. Cheri had opinions. They were like the opinions most fifteen-year-olds have, bless her heart, but Tim presented them in a tone so reverential it was as if Cheri herself had carved them into the cedars of Lebanon. War, Cheri had figured out, was bad. Hunting was also bad. If humans had guns, the animals should, too. You should be allowed to smoke in school because if smoking were allowed in school there would be a lot less skipping of school. If parents hadn't forgotten what it was like to be young, the world would be a better place. And so on. I thought if old Chairman Mao (I'd read about him in college) had heard some of these gems, he'd have tossed his little red book into the Yangtze River.

But a rare gem of my own in an otherwise rough field of social skills was the ability to mind my own business. So, while Tim talked about Cheri, I'd merely listen. On the love front, I was a loyal listener. Tim wanted to believe that it was possible to find love among the bleak sawdust hills of Lake City, Michigan, and I'd be darned before I'd remove even one shovel full of hope.

For Tim was pinched. We were all pinched in one way or another, but you could see it had really fastened on him. His early life seemed to have been one big pinch, and his mill life was hardly a reprieve. Inside the fence the gears of the machinery were waiting to pinch your fingers purple if not all the way off. You could pinch your toes when kicking stacks into symmetry, and if you leaned in too close you could pinch your belly (or worse) when banding a stack of cants. There was the pinch of cigarettes between fingers, safety glasses on nose bridges, and, though it was rare, new boots on tender feet (new boots being the rare part). There was the pinch between your paycheck and the electric bill and the pinch between late, late nights and bleary-eyed mornings; there was the past forever pinching the future. In his pursuit of love, Tim was only trying to pry the pinch apart. So I'd listen to him talk about Cheri all morning, and then I'd walk out to the truck at break time, where Randy would ask for the reading on the Cheri-meter. The Cheri-meter was the Richter scale of Whiskey-Tim's Cheri talk.

"A ten," I'd complain, and then I'd curse. Randy, of course, would laugh.

But as bad as it was for us on the chain—and some days my head was a throbbing blob of Cheriness—for Tim it was worse. He was fooling himself with this girl, and he knew it. When his river of heartsick, rising all spring, finally toppled him into the rapids, it bounced his head off a couple of logs, a head already so mixed up with beer, speed, marijuana, and his unrequited love for Cheri that even the most sophisticated psychological pike pole couldn't have saved him. So confused had he become that he even allowed the Tattoo Man to needle an inky blotch on his forearm before the Tattoo Man himself logged out of the mill forever. That Tim was so taken with this tattoo was a sign that the sluice gate had burst.

The morning after his rendezvous with the needles, Tim walked through the big sliding door, his thorny grin as wide as daybreak. He rolled up his sleeve and held out his arm as if I were his grandpa and he was showing me where the doctor had given him the measles shot. If only the pokes had been good for him. There, on the back of his forearm in greenish ink, was a Jack Daniels label. In place of the words "No. 7 Brand" were two words with a hyphen: Whiskey-Tim. A copyright violation aside, the artwork was even sloppier than what the Tattoo Man had lavished on himself (more on that later).

"He was a little high when he did it," Whiskey-Tim said, "but it's not that bad."

Having a tattoo that was "not that bad" was like having a maple fall on you instead of an oak.

"Is that real or did he draw it on first?" I asked, trying not to wince.

"It's real," Tim said. "He did it for free."

I then asked something I'd sworn prostrate at the foot of the Great Golden Sawdust Mountain I would never ask. "What does Cheri think?"

Tim managed a coy grin. "She thinks he's mutilated my arm," he said.

The girl's bluntness was somehow touching. Maybe all the free beer and cigarettes were finally adding up to a concerned candor or maybe they were building up to the brush-off, which might have been the same thing. And maybe Tim sensed it. Whatever the origin, from that point on his behavior was that of a frustrated man. He'd stay out till all hours of the morning, mixing beer, marijuana, and diet pills, then show up late for work, bragging about his indulgences, his eyes red as paint fire. Bristling through his exhaustion, he'd chide the older workers for their dedication to the mill and then chide the new men for their inexperience. In calmer moments he'd curse the wood, the weather, and any semblance of authority no matter how benign. Whiskey-Tim the elf had become Whiskey-Tim the troll.

One night his mother kicked him out of the house for rowdiness—another crisp explanation—and Whiskey-Tim spent the night walking sidewalks and dodging the police. In a less cheery personality such a domestic squabble might have triggered a bank-robbing spree or worse, but for Tim it was just another story to tell in the morning in lieu of stacking the wood.

As spring wore on, he was absent from the mill a day or two weekly, laughing off the manager's reprimands. Hung over, his march down Bacon Street became more labored, his move for the next cant on the green chains less eager. He crowned his frequent tardiness with half-hour bathroom breaks, claiming he had diarrhea and leaving the bulk of the stacking to me. I kept my tongue, thinking the bathroom breaks of a man who had spent eighteen months in the pen for stealing commodes was a delicate subject best left enthroned. Besides, I couldn't forget it was Whiskey-Tim who had taught me the technique, was the first to shake my hand, and had more than held up his end of hours of conversation. Along with Randy, he had made the mill bearable.

Between cants one morning he told me he was cutting back on his partying so he could save money to buy a ring for Cheri. He figured if he put away a paycheck or two he could afford a little diamond that would suit her just fine. Her parents were hassling her for smoking cigarettes and skipping school, and Tim's aim was to rescue her. As he stared uneasily through the big entrance, he told me the moment she turned sixteen he planned to propose marriage. I doubted he believed this himself, that it was just the empty trill of a man whose heart had been run over by a forklift, a man who had had the last fetter squeezed off his desperation.

His frazzled state of mind was evident the next morning when he lumbered up along the wood chip van, favoring his non-tattooed arm. Even on his most lovelorn days, Tim always managed to bid me good morning, but that morning he stuck to the end of the chain, quiet as a mud clump. The

air was heavy with the smell of damp sawdust and forklift ex-
haust, and Tim moved as if a large sandbag had been placed
across his shoulders. He was able to stack a pine board or two
with his wounded wing, but when a snag on the chain
seemed to get the better of him I went down to help.

"What's up?" I asked.

Tim said, "Not much," and we fixed the snag and stood
there.

"Did you hurt your arm?"

Whiskey-Tim wasn't used to reticence. With the nudge
he was out from under it quicker than a bug from beneath
plywood. When he held out the arm, I could see on the
underflesh of his forearm three burn wounds the size of
quarters; dark streaks of infection spidered up to the crook
of his elbow from all three.

"I bet Cheri she could put out her cigarette on my arm
and I wouldn't budge," he said.

Cheri had taken him up on it, the third time pulling the
cigarette away, claiming she couldn't do it anymore.

"She told me she loved me too much," Tim said. He tried
to sound upbeat, but his eyes were flat with despair.

That afternoon, as he sat on a stack of popple boards
staring at nothing, I decided I should say something. I started
down the green chains toward him but hesitated. I started
again, hesitated again. I don't know why I hesitated except
that sometimes when you're about to do the right thing you
hesitate. It felt like I was about to swipe the Cracker Jack
from a little boy at a ball game, but somebody had to say
something. When finally I was standing next to him, Tim
looked up and smiled a bit, expectant.

I pointed to his arm. "Anyone who does that to you," I said, "doesn't love you."

Whiskey-Tim nodded. "I know," he said. And he seemed relieved to admit it.

A few weeks later Tim was fired for taking his paycheck from the manager's desk a day before payday. He was fired on the spot before we had a chance to say good-bye. He left town soon after, and the last we heard he was working on a garbage truck downstate. I could picture that: Whiskey-Tim hanging off the back of a roaring truck, riding the wind as it whistled through his gap-toothed grin, an elf again, happy again.

For several weeks that spring I missed him as though he had died.

THE BLANCHED ONE

NOW AND THEN Blanched Duane pops up in my memory like one of those bothersome protein squiggles dancing in your line of sight. A punchy bantamweight of eighteen, Duane emitted such a sour attitude that I have tried to forget him, but there he stands, reminding me that his contribution to my education, while brief, was fairly pointed.

I remember Duane chiefly for his ascent one cold spring morning to the platform of the nailing machine, where he began to crow that we were all fools for working so hard for so little pay. The north end of the sawmill was dark and cold and possessed the acoustics of a toolshed, but there stood Duane on high, his spine and legs thin as chicken wire, dressed in a white T-shirt and white painter's pants, his blond, almost white hair spiked below the rim of his white hard hat, delivering his message with such fury you figured the color of rage was, well, white.

It was evident that Blanched Duane was appalled to have found himself working among so many in desperate need of enlightenment. It was also apparent that the opening to ascend the platform so he could shine his sage light down on us was too tempting to resist.

The trouble was Duane had climbed on his soapbox just as break time was beginning, and everyone knows even a burlesque show couldn't hold a workingman's attention then (I exaggerate a mite, but you get the idea). All we could do was shake our heads at Duane's obvious words, curl a sucker grin in his direction, and keep walking.

Poor Duane looked at the sea of turned backs, dropped his shoulders, and stood dumbfounded. He then marched out to his white van, drove off to blow off some steam, came back morose as a toad, and sulked for the rest of the afternoon. Now and then he'd look up and scan the mill with a sneer just to let us know our rebuff had been hurtful. A few days later he climbed into his van and left the sawmill forever.

With so much energy to expend, it's almost a sure bet that Duane would have been a river hog during the heyday of the lumberman. Easy to picture him on a swift stretch of the Muskegon River, hot-stepping from log to log, challenging the very cuss in himself not to stumble. Out there with a pike pole to steady himself, he would have burned up the anger that in 1980 was burning him up and had put what little red was in his cheeks.

On days when Randy was absent, I'd sometimes hitch a ride home with Duane. During these rides Duane drove like a maniac, passing every vehicle in sight (even in "no-passing" zones, where, with his elbows out, his chest and chin an inch from the wheel, and his eyes bugged to the windshield, he'd muse "What are the odds?"). After a couple of white-knuckled trips, I decided that Duane viewed the world as one big rat race and his intention was to overtake it as fast as he could, thereby avoiding the suckers, the pluckers, and the weak willed. His driving was a harrowing manifestation of this philosophy. If given a chance I'm sure he would have passed the governor of the great state of Michigan (police escort and all) on a muddy dirt road just to thumb his attitude toward the world.

Duane's gift to my sawmill education was his platform speech, which showed me that even a ridiculous presentation can hold the truth. Indeed, on break that morning, after telling Randy about the Blanched One's tirade—stretching my neck like a rooster as Duane had done and mimicking his rabbled tone—I settled into a lull and decided Duane was right: too much work, too little pay. Later I reflected that Duane was right about us settling for so little pay but wrong about us working too hard. The first is a matter of economics, the second—much more important—a matter of spirit, which Duane had in abundance in his own way and should not have criticized in others.

I didn't share Duane's impulse to hop onto any kind of box and spout my gripes about the mill, although I can't deny that my list of improvements was always at the ready: a drinking fountain in the mill, longer break times, hard hats with cushy suspension, free Cokes and snacks in the break room, and so on. It was a list, in other words, as about as viable as the campaign promises of a seventh-grade student council election, although I think Duane would have approved of it.

But I didn't climb onto the soapbox because the truth is that at the sawmill, complaints fell into the same category as ballet: unrecognized. The mill was a take it or leave it proposition. Reformers need not apply, although they often did and often went the way of Blanched Duane, who was obviously wounded by not having brought the masses to heel. Still, the lesson that there was more than one way to make your point about nearly anything was born of Duane's antics, and he deserves credit for it.

In my memory he's an inch taller this year than he was last year.

ROUTINE

O N MY WORKTABLE is a panorama of the lumber town of Michelson, Michigan, circa 1910. As with many progressive era photographs, the exposure is overly bright, yet it manages to capture the weariness, the bareknuckled bleakness, of a small and often snowbound company town. Michelson is now under the backwaters of the Reedsburg Dam near Houghton Lake, but in its day it was a place of neatly framed clapboard structures, a dozen along each side of Main Street, including the boardinghouse, the telegraph office, and the company store. With the mill in the background, the buildings suggest routine and discipline, reminding me of the mix of reluctance and necessity with which I used to view such values when I was twenty years old. They also remind me of the house I lived in just up the road from Michelson and my own routine during my sawmill days.

It was a hollow-walled place no bigger than a company house that I shared with at least three generations of mice and later with the mice and a young wife. My wife and the mice did not get along. I suppose I should have seen this coming, but I was young myself and still unaware that my domestic vision lacked nuance. Soon after my wife set down her bags, however, it became clear that I should buy a mousetrap.

This was a balanced enough move, but then I bought little sticker stars to put on the trap whenever the trap caught a mouse. A big mouse earned a gold star, a small mouse a red or a blue star, depending on my mood. Probably I should have seen this for the flippancy it was, for my wife didn't find it funny in the least, and I'm almost sure the mice didn't either. But then I was young and by then, ask anyone, aging rapidly.

My independent feeling was that the mice were harmless little rascals that helped with the lack of insulation by shifting windward in the walls, provided my pounding was insistent enough. At the time I didn't know a company house from a condominium, but my thought was that this drafty house, the conflict between my wife and the mice, and the scratching of the big maple on the north side of the house on windy nights, which only somewhat muted the stertorous barking of the neighbor's huge Labrador retriever, was what I deserved for dropping out of college.

The photograph of Michelson reveals only a few trees within the town limits and not a dog in sight, although I'm sure squeamish souls and mice are lurking somewhere.

Ah, but in a house of conflict there is solace in routine. At 6:55 each morning my feet would drop onto the cold linoleum of the bedroom floor, and as I stooped to pull on my ragged work clothing, heaped by the bed where I'd let it fall the night before, I'd be wide awake, for not even the strongest

coffee matches cold linoleum as an aphrodisiac for wakeful-
ness. After brushing my teeth, I'd tug on my boots, grab a
cookie from the jar and a Coca-Cola from the refrigerator—
a combination I thought of as the stacker's breakfast—and
then, precisely at 7:03, Randy would pull up in his Blazer
and, with old Bob the maintenance man riding shotgun, we
would start out on the twenty-five-mile drive to the sawmill.

I'd loll in the backseat, feeling the subtle shifts and turns
of the journey as we wound down Route 55 through the
Dead Stream Swamp, crossed the Muskegon River, and
droned past our ancestral home of Merritt. We would bore
past Merritt Speedway (Action Track of the North!), streak
across the pine plains near Keelan Corners, ease down the
Canfield Rise, and finally roll into the eastern edge of Lake
City about the time the moon went from a dim nightlight to
a faded aspirin pill. At Bacon Street we would hang a left,
then a quick right, and wheel into the parking lot.

It was when I climbed out into the frosted dawn and was
following Randy through the ditch along Bacon that I felt it.
High in my triceps and behind my knees, the muscle, the
joint cartilage, pulled like taffy, a good two inches longer
than the previous day: I was taller.

Now I'll admit that this infliction, if it could be called
that, was partly psychosomatic, for on the drive out to the
mill, sprawled in the backseat listening to the static voices on
WQON-FM and the less electric chatter between old Bob
and Randy, I certainly felt my normal size. It was only when
I leaned up and glimpsed the mill—a modern day manifestation of a medieval torture rack—only then did I feel

stretched. At first it was unsettling, like being followed by a bee. But later it wasn't so bad. Most mornings I liked the idea of being taller.

SCRUFF SCUFFLE

O NE MORNING Whiskey-Tim snuck off to the dentist, leaving me alone on the chains with a birdish man named Schultzie. Schultzie was twenty-four years old and possessed a throat contoured like a rutted road and a sullen demeanor every dip as bumpy. As the new man, I deferred to his seniority (for all of two weeks, a virtual epoch on the green chains) and stacked the cants, which allowed Schultzie to monitor them for snags. Monitoring for snags was a simple job of desnagging the boards and cants that sometimes hung up on the chain like tree limbs or drunken canoeists on a river. When I told Schultzie I would do the stacking, he gave me a "damn right you will" nod and doddered around to the other side of the chain. So much for deference.

Contrary to the impression I've probably left so far, you had to have abilities to work in the sawmill. At least one of the following was vital: the ability to stack heavy lumber; the ability to add witty substance to the morning coffee gathering in the break room; or the ability to accept teasing of any kind, which included criticism of your appearance and verbal denigration of your hometown, automobile, and significant other. Schultzie lacked all of these abilities, which must have made his work day feel longer than a train ride to Lapland.

In the heyday of the logging era, Schultzie would have been the cook's assistant, and he would have made a glum one. In those days, the dining hour was supposed to be as quiet as deer feeding in a meadow, and one look at the grim set of Schultzie's jaw would have set a lumberjack to contemplating the finer aspects of man's troubled nature and thereby ensured silence for the duration of the meal.

Despite Schultzie's prickliness, the morning was going smoothly when an oak slab suddenly upended between two chains and stood straight as a sentry. I waited for Schultzie to pounce, but when he didn't I called his name through the roar and pointed. Schultzie pointed back but with a different finger than I'd used, indicating (and this is a loose interpretation) that I was number one. Such a high-held position, however, was in some place other than his heart, and with his finger still in the air he began to shout names at me, including the usual dazzler that one had had an incestuous relationship with one's mother.

This particular appellation has served more notice than any dinner bell ever rung. In fact, the words, with their levitating power, caused Shultzie to sneer, which squared his jaw and knuckled his forehead and made him seem taller and broader than he was. I could see danger in the sneer; the trouble was I didn't know how much. All I knew was that his glare, pinned back and outraged, seemed to be trying to

burn a hole right through me. Deference had just been murdered with a torch.

Nobody was looking, so I decided to throw my hard hat
at him. I flung it across the green chains, half Frisbee, half
fastball, and Schultzie ducked. If he hadn't, I'm sure the hard
hat would have clipped him in that shin guard of a throat
and ended the misery of many. Still no one seemed to be
looking, so I crawled up on the first chain and took the chains
one by one as you might use stones to cross a river. I'd no
more than landed on the other side when three of my coworkers grabbed me, the riot squad as it were.

A mumbled warning to calm down was dropped in my
ear, so I took a deep breath, composed myself, and slowly
walked back around the chain, willing to forget the whole
thing. The anger was almost gone when Schultzie suddenly
appeared next to me. He had hightailed it back to the tool-
room wall and cowered there until the danger had passed.
Now, having recovered his courage, he was standing with his
nose six inches from mine, telling me he wanted to fight me
after work, a threat that knotted my already nervous stomach tighter than the root of a box elder tree.

To predict what would happen next was as easy as reading the funny paper. Word of the fight would buzz through
the mill all day, and at quitting time the crew would gather
outside the gate to watch the freak show. With the craving
for depraved entertainment as insatiable at the sawmill as
anywhere else, I decided it made no sense to put it off.

"We're not going to wait that long," I told Schultzie, and
the depravity commenced. Legend has it that in bygone logging days fighting was common among men with names

like Dagger Bob, Ax Bit Al, and Stump Jaw Jones, their fisti-
cuffs raging hour upon bloody hour before one of the noble
warriors finally succumbed to exhaustion. This was nothing
like that. The end result, which came quickly, was that the
riot squad (who had arrived too late this time) had to help
Schultzie into the break room to clean him up. One of these
men, his eyes wide with wariness, came back to the mill to
assure me that the manager would soon catch wind of the
fight and I'd be fired. I thanked him for his prophecy (false,
it turned out) and told him not to get my hopes up.

In the truck at break time, Randy couldn't stop laughing.
Skinny Eddie had gone up to his saw booth and told him
all about the fight, and as I sat scrunched and hunched—a
beast in a bucket seat—Randy yipped like a coyote at a
duckling parade. As I brooded, I remembered a fight between the foreman of my first sawmill and a new employee
who had committed the sawdust sin of stacking a pallet in
the wrong place. The manager, a wiry man with the build
and ferocity of Blanched Duane, was suddenly so far into
the man's face you couldn't have slipped a handkerchief between them. In a flash the new man, a stocky fellow, had the
foreman pinned to the ground and was about to bloody his
face when a couple of the hands pulled him off. The man was
fired, of course, although it wasn't evident that he was entirely at fault.

I was appalled that in my first foray into the working
world of adults I had been given a front-row seat to such
immaturity. It smacked so loudly of the playground that
I wanted to bury my head in a sandbox. My comment
to Randy at the time was that it was correct to make the

arbitrary age of eighteen the definition of adulthood, for to base it on behavior would have been too much of a crap-shoot. It was the kind of mindless philosophizing you do after a couple of cold beers on an empty stomach, and I recall Randy being mildly amused at my disgust, though all he said was "The world is complicated." Now, a mere two years later, I had gone from disgusted to disgusting with one punch.

When Randy (still laughing) paused to catch his breath, I told him Schultzie had returned to the mill, a bandage over his brow, and apologized. The poor scruff (we were all poor scruffs) hadn't thought I'd get so angry.

"What did you say to him?" Randy asked.

"I said, 'What did you expect?'" I answered, not funny words, but Randy laughed at length again and then pointed out the bright side. Now that I'd proven I could handle my-self, I would never have to fight at the mill again (true enough).

Nevertheless, the self-disappointment clogged me in ways sawdust never could. Brawling was legendary during the heyday of the lumbering era, but a hundred years later I felt less a legend than a lout.

"Now," Randy said, "you have a reputation."

An image sprung to mind, shadowy and unsavory, and I turned away from it. "Yeah," I mumbled into the window, "I'm a barbarian."

Schultzie's anger lingers heavily in my memory, but his lithe figure is never quite brawny enough for my conscience.

YULETIDE BLUR

THE AFTERNOON OF THE CHRISTMAS PARTY is a blur. I remember frozen turkeys handed out from the back of the company pickup to a line of weary men who had worked at the mill three months or longer. I remember mumbled thank-yous, the usual outbreak of navel gazing, smiles indistinguishable from grimaces, and the line growing shorter and shorter until all that remained in that run of the mill yard was the iron chill of a winter dusk. I remember the disappointment I felt, knowing that, with only a few days of duty at the mill, I was ineligible for the culinary part of the Yuletide extravaganza, but how I brightened when I was invited to a local watering hole, underage though I was, to take advantage of the two-hundred-dollar tab the owner of the mill had set up for those wanting to indulge their holiday spirit. I remember sitting in the Blazer with the turkeys belonging to Randy and old Bob the maintenance man on either side of me as we drove quietly, and, if memory serves, rather quickly, to the bar. I remember sitting in a narrow chair in a dim lounge thinking, "I'm sitting in a narrow chair in a dim lounge." Soon after is when it really gets blurry.

I remember the barmaid being suspicious of my age but spotting me two beers before she decided to check my ID. I remember her anger at finding I was two months shy of being old enough to drink but saying I could stay in the bar as long as I behaved myself. I remember thinking—with cold, clear self-assessment—that abstinence was about as likely as one of those frozen turkeys turning into a condor.

A short time after my promise to be good, the one we called the Tattoo Man arrived and began pushing me Kessler's and Coke, a combination that set a mist before my eye and a song in my heart. I remember that the good cheer was sapped when it was announced the tab had been spent but that the mood revived when the wallets of the rank and file were pulled out and parted. I remember wanting to buy a round for the boys but having only my paycheck and no open bank close by to liquidate it. I remember Russy, the mill's dark-bearded mechanic, saying he could cash it, me asking if he was sure, Russy saying the green-chainer check hadn't been printed that he couldn't cash, and everyone laughing. Sometime after that I remember the barmaid telling me in a very firm voice that if I didn't leave the premises at once I'd be talking to the police.

The next thing I knew I was sitting with the turkeys again. Big snowflakes were lightly thudding the windows. I was telling the turkeys that I realized America had other ideas for its youth besides stacking lumber, namely, collegiate, entrepreneurial, military, or missionary ideas, but someday— and now I was shouting and jabbing my finger into the air— someday my brothers, believe you me, I would rise above those mounds of sawdust, I would shed these rags and callused hands, I'd . . . There was a tapping at the window. I wiped a spot clear in the fogged glass and looked out to see the manager's bearded face looking back. I practically fell out of the truck to see him standing with old Bob and Randy. The crew was soused.

Apparently, intoxication can alter one's hearing, for I clearly heard the manager ask me how old I was, the first question he'd ever asked that I understood.

"Twenty," I said. "Twenty-one early next year."

"When?"

"February."

"Well, then, you're not old enough to drink."

"No . . . Yes . . . I'm not."

The manager held up the keys to Randy's truck. "Then you drive."

Maybe you had to be drunk to understand such logic, but there it was. We told the manager he was the best boss we'd ever had and piled our maudlin arses into the truck. I drove, or something like it, to Merritt and then on to Houghton Lake. I jump ahead to let you know we made it. At our parents' house in Merritt (we needed to use the facilities) I ran over a couple of the railroad ties that lined the driveway, bouncing old Bob (back with the turkeys) so high off the seat his head hit the ceiling, which explains a fragment of memory that includes loud cursing. Later he said the top of his head was sore for a month and he was sure the button atop his cap had been pushed a quarter inch into his skull.

So that was Christmas at the sawmill as seen through memory's dehydrated lens. I'm ashamed that I mixed drinking and driving and feel it acutely even now. Whenever I recall that afternoon, it comes back in a sequence of drunken scenes, each one as dim as a faded daguerreotype, a bad act that might have easily ended in disaster. Thankfully, the only repercussion was having to listen to old Bob tell me for the rest of the winter that he couldn't wait until I was old enough to drink and not drive.

THE CAT

HE WAS TALL, gangly, and forever grinning one of those grins you give a double take because the first glance hasn't told you whether the grinner is daft or dangerous. Our friend the Cat was not daft, but, not altogether purposely, he may have been dangerous.

The Cat was six foot four and 210 rangy pounds, the wrong size for instability. He wore a handsome handlebar mustache bent over a mouthful of rotten teeth and pulled the bill of his cap, creased in five places, low over his laughing eyes. He wore big stompin' boots and tucked a drop-chain wallet in the hip pocket of his jeans, the bank of the hard collars. Arms, legs, smile, everything about the Cat moved easily but landed with the subtlety of iron. To look up into the dark slot that folded bill made of his eyes was to feel the stare of menace. The Cat had the dimensions to hurt people. Now and then he did.

Randy had known the Cat for years and sometimes drank with him. One Friday night he watched the Cat beat up two men outside a bar in Houghton Lake Heights. The Cat kicked one man in the head with his big boot after he'd felled him with a punch and beat the other with the radio antenna he'd snapped off the man's car. True defeat, Randy said, was being whipped with your own car antenna. He told me the man had crawled across the gravel, begging for his life, while the Cat stood over him laughing, joyous as a seven-year-old pulling the wings off a fly.

"No doubt about it," said Randy in a tone strung between admiration and apocalypse, "the Cat is a nasty son of a bitch."

I'm not sure what kind of job the Cat would have had during the lumberman's heyday—with his long legs he might have covered a lot of ground as a timber cruiser—but there's no doubt he would have been a brawler of note. On weekends he would have paddled across the Straits of Mackinac and pierced the dense Upper Peninsula forest all the way to Seney, the toughest mill town in logging lore. There he would have punched the lights out of Silver Jack Discroll, flattened Fast Freddy Felton, and thumped Brawling Billy Brass to within an inch of their lives. With his work done in Seney, he would have moved on to Ishpeming and Negaunee to whip a renegade miner or two.

As I observed the Cat with guilty admiration, I realized something about myself. It occurred to me that while swatting Schultzie had helped my reputation, I wasn't really cut out to be a tough guy. The Cat liked a good joke and a funny story, but he had also bent the bill of his cap in five places as if to give notice that he possessed many edges, most of them sharp. I had neither a mental nor a physical swagger, and truly tough guys have both. The bill of my cap was arched like a quarter moon and said "harmless" if it said anything. That my smile was flat and timid instead of curl lipped and cocky would have turned me out of the tough guy ranks early. In those days I had impressive biceps and forearms, but my slouched posture seemed better suited for bending over a book at a table than for boxing the ears of a big mouth. The only reputation I really wanted anyway was that of someone who minded his own business. I was nothing like the Cat, but then, in his heart, the Cat was nothing like the Cat either.

He could be playful. His mustache spread like welcoming arms when he smiled, when some mischievousness overtook his mind. One morning he went out behind the mill, snatched up a grasshopper the size of a clothespin, and stuffed it into a bottle of green Chloraseptic one of our unsuspecting mates had brought in to spray down his throat, which was raw and sore from a night of drinking. All morning we watched the man unwittingly take the bottle from a shelf and squirt his tonsils until he could swallow without wincing. Once in a while the Cat would sneak over and hold up the bottle, and there would be the grasshopper, looking back through the murk in the same way we looked at the world: sadly and more than a little dazed.

At break time one day, I asked Randy how the Cat got his nickname.

"A poker game," Randy said. "Ran out of money and bet if he lost the next hand he'd bite the jugular of a kitten that was hanging around the table."

This card game had taken place a couple of years earlier in a small resort cabin Randy and his bride had rented near Houghton Lake. The kitty in question was a stray that had wandered in for attention. As Randy told it, the Cat indeed lost the hand, scooped up the kitty, and began to gnaw. Enough wailing and hissing to scar the eardrums had pierced the cabin air before the kitten went silent and passed out. The Cat, his mouth full of hair and his cheek stung from a two-pronged scratch, lay his victim down and, in an apparent act of telepathy, stared wild-eyed at the kitten until it revived. The poor thing tottered a bit afterward but was fine. Randy said the Cat wanted to put on a tough front about it all, but when the party broke up he gathered the kitty and coddled and cuddled it until it was fully on its paws again, eight lives left to live. After hearing this story, the Cat so finally became "the Cat" in my mind that I had to pause in order to recall his real name.

Occasionally, we gave the Cat a lift home from work. Each time, on the way out of town, we would stop at the Trading Post Party Store, where the Cat would pull several grubby dollars from that drop-chain wallet to buy a small bottle of Black Velvet whiskey and a cold 7UP. Then, in the backseat of the Blazer, he'd concoct his drink in a Styrofoam cup, lift the mix in a toast, and say, "Gotta have snake juice."

My guess is that snake juice, and a possible case of cat scratch fever, caused any number of behavioral aberrations. One blustery afternoon Randy and I visited Cat in his apartment, a sparsely furnished duplex on a winding road across from Houghton Lake. The Cat gave us the grand tour, the last stop being the bedroom, where a bazooka lay on the floor near the wall. Because it was the Cat's house, we weren't necessarily shocked, although it was strange as snow in June to see a bazooka nestled in the carpet of nonmilitary quarters. The Cat's explanation was that he'd found the bazooka in a field near Camp Grayling, a national guard base twenty miles to the north. Of course "found" was a euphemism for stolen, and we guessed the field was more than adjacent to the camp, but we kept our geographical musings to ourselves. Tramping through the moonlight with the thing over his shoulder, the Cat was sure he'd be caught, although why he'd worried about being caught after "finding" something was another thing we didn't ask. The Cat stared admiringly at the weapon and said, "One of these nights I'm going back for the shells." That was our last visit to the stockpile.

From the Cat's example I learned that the glue that holds a tough exterior in place sometimes gives way, which is to say the toughness is a front or at least much of it is. It is not to say the tough aren't tough underneath, just that sometimes there's a thread or two of tenderness as well.

I remember the morning a chunk of metal shot from a log Red Eye was sawing and caught Randy on the chin as he came down the steps of his booth. I remember him coming through the side door of the mill, the bottom half of his face bearded in blood from a gash that would require six stitches to close. I remember running toward him as if in slow motion when suddenly someone bolted past me. It was the Cat. He was running so hard to help that he staggered and nearly fell. It was a spasm of human concern, that stagger, and because of it I'm forever convinced the Cat never intended to harm that kitty, never intended to fire a bazooka shell across Houghton Lake, and never intended for his tough guy image to get out of hand, though maybe it had. And later, when he had a skull tattooed on his chest to go with the various medieval-looking critters on his forearms, when it seemed the tough front was hardening inward, another memory would come to me: the Cat climbing onto the school bus when he was a senior in high school. He was a year ahead of me, we lived in the same neighborhood, and I still see him mounting the bus steps and easing his lanky frame into the front seat. His hair was trimmed, he wore a spring jacket of pale yellow, and his expression was that of shy person. He was so serious and thoughtful that he might have been a quiet honor student bound for Princeton. I thought he looked like an accounting major.

THE STACKER

SOMETIMES IT TAKES flipping through a frayed book or two or staring at the wall in a small-town museum, but the ocean of photographs from the lumbering era is well stocked and eventually I see someone who might have been me: a weary, stoop-shouldered, troubled-seeming young man standing with his arms at his sides, his head bent in muddled thought. It feels odd, the older stacker (as I think of myself) looking down at the younger. The look on that youthful face belongs to someone with a bit or two to grind, a face from the time when I stood in the bleak light of the big mill entrance feeling not young and carefree but withered and timid and disappointed that almost without effort I'd become a lumber stacker. To hear the words *lumber stacker* made my existence sound so low, so paltry, that its worth in sand would have hardly filled a grub hole.

A lumber stacker. Not a wood location engineer, not even a manager of reduced deciduous elements . . . *A lumber stacker*.

It had less resonance than *ditchdigger*, not to mention half the pay.

There was no doubt in my dusty mind that all the other twenty-year-olds in America were in far better straits. I imagined them in polo shirts with beauty shop haircuts and bodies muscled by machinery in carpeted gyms. I imagined disco music, smooth gyrations, and gleaming white teeth. I was disappointed in whatever mysterious authority allowed such shallowness to be so important, yet I yearned to wallow in it myself. Whenever I looked down I was ashamed of my torn jacket, my patched, threadbare trousers, and my worn work boots; I was even ashamed of the calluses on my hands, the ridges of which were large enough to jam a pencil stub through. I felt better only when I remembered that I'd come from a long line of blue-collar workers who had themselves descended from farmers—strong, American peasant stock is how I thought of us—and that implicit in the strength I used to hoist the wood was the hardiness, with its elements of sentimentality and naïveté, that would get me through the short time I planned to stay at the mill.

It comforted me to remember my father and his fellow mechanics as they squatted on the concrete drive of the garage at the north end of Lansing, the capital city, where we had moved from tiny Merritt so my father could find work to support a wife and seven kids (we later moved back to Merritt). He and the other mechanics would be dressed in their rental shades-of-blue uniforms and oil-blackened work boots, gazing toward downtown with its skyline of office buildings and smokestacks, sipping beer and smoking cigarettes on a Saturday afternoon, the workweek finally over. They would talk about carburetors and radiators, baseball, the tread on semitruck tires, and all the deer they had ever shot, gutted, and eaten in their lives. Now and then you would hear a shout in the neighborhood, a screen door clapping shut, or a motorcycle sputtering in the distance. When these sounds came, there would be a pause in the conversation, and palpable in the silence, before the talk moved on to bird dogs and spark plugs, was the satisfaction of men who had earned their rest. As I stood in the big mill entrance, wiping the sawdust from my eyes, it was a comfort to know that I, too, had earned a few sweet moments of reprieve.

THE INNOCENT

B E CAREFUL WHAT YOU SAY in front of Lanny Boy,"
Randy warned one morning as we drove to the mill.
"What for?" I asked.

"He's the company spy."

At the sawmill to be a company man was akin to being a
fascist, but to be the company spy was akin to being a fascist
rat. It may be that there were real vermin and a fascist or two
around the sawmill, but I couldn't bend Lanny into either
category. During my first weeks at the mill he would often
wander down from the north end where the pallets were
built, grab a cant off the chain, and, with what can only be
described as grizzly strength, manhandle it onto a stack. The
extent of our first conversation was Lanny asking if I was
Randy's brother and me confirming it. Name, rank, and
serial number only, I cautioned myself, but I quickly tossed
all concerns aside.

If Lanny was a spy, if he was toting information back to
the manager that could later be used to compromise the employment of a coworker, he was oblivious to it. To Lanny all
talk was small talk, the only kind he knew. If you said it out
loud, it must mean you didn't care if it was repeated, sound

logic, literally. In fact he believed your reason for saying it was so it could be repeated; thus, we would learn more about one another and grow closer. Lanny Boy, not Whiskey-Tim, was the sawmill innocent.

He loved disco and Elvis for crying out loud! He smoked cigarettes to be cool and blew smoke rings to be cooler still. His hair was permed into tight curls, and he donned polyester shirts and fake gold chains beneath his canvas coveralls. Saturday nights, in thrall among thirteen- and fourteen-year-olds, he danced at the local kiddie disco. The sea of youth parted for him just as it did for John Travolta in *Saturday Night Fever*, or so Lanny claimed. No, he wasn't a spy. The worst thing about Lanny was a pinch of arrogance.

He was proud to have worked at the mill since he was sixteen, five eager years, the longest stint of anyone except old Henry, who had been operating the cutoff saw since at least the end of the iron age. Pride and the sawmill were not easy to meld, but, like Henry, Lanny had done it. He'd come to the mill as a co-op student, walking over from the high school each weekday afternoon. Lanny crossed those furlongs to the mill with his head held high, but it's doubtful many of his classmates would have.

Sometimes, between employments of the technique, I would gaze toward the school through the big sliding door and imagine the class rowdy being rousted from the back row of study hall by the assistant principal. I imagined him being led down the hallway and nudged out the back double doors into the parking lot, where the AP would turn him due east so he was facing the sawmill. Then, in words drenched with doom, the AP would say, "That's where you'll end up if you don't behave yourself." The boy would begin to tremble. His Adam's apple would hop like a bobber on a wild lake. In short, he'd be scared and know it. He might not become a Rhodes scholar, or even the local Elk's Club scholarship winner, but that one portentous glimpse of the mill would rattle his brain fenders enough that he'd at least give good behavior a thought.

But Lanny came gladly. The young shanty boy quickly became the pet of the older workers, all of whom teased and cajoled him on his journey from sawdust novice to experienced mill hand. When I knew him he even talked like someone who had worked in a loud sawmill for half a decade—through the side of his mouth, swiveling his lips and chin muscles down to his jawbone to funnel his words through the thunderous noise—as if it were 1932, you were a federal agent on a stakeout, and Lanny was whispering very calmly but with great gravity that the Canadians had just crossed the border with the whiskey.

Through this same mouth he bragged that he had more longevity at the mill than even Randy. "Yeah," I said, "but he's a sawyer, and we're peons," words that brought Lanny's spine erect and set him to spouting a list of his talents. He had, he stated flatly (if not flatulently), operated the forklift, the cutoff saw, the nailer, and the notcher; toiled on the green chain; and run errands for the manager.

"I've done it all," he said. "I'm a whatchamacallit. A jack . . . a jack . . ."

"A jackass?"

"No. A jack-of-all-trades," he said. And with that he smacked his lips as if self-satisfaction were a big piece of chocolate cake.

But the thing about Lanny Boy wasn't the enormity of his sawmill talent; the thing about Lanny was Elvis. To know what frosted the Lanny cake was to know that for him the King was king. One morning he hopped off the forklift, ignoring a stack of popple cants waiting to be moved, just to ask what kind of music I liked. I slid a board onto a stack, straightened up, and gave it a thought.

"I guess the usual stuff you hear on the radio," I told him.

"You like Elvis?" Lanny asked.

"Some of it. . . . I hear you love him." Lanny's worship of Elvis had long been mill lore.

"What about it?" he said, frowning. "There's nothing wrong with it."

He blew a smoke ring through his sidewinder mouth and blinked. His eyes, soaked in hurt, were pink at the rims. I gulped back an opinion about blasphemy and agreed there wasn't a thing wrong with it. To make Lanny feel better, I mentioned that my mom and dad and Elvis had all been born the same year and that my dad often said Elvis could sing anything: country, gospel, rock and roll, and, if the Furies poked him just right, probably opera, too.

Lanny nodded militantly and said, "Your dad's a smart man."

He drew big on his cigarette, blew out another smoke ring, and sent a punch through the middle of it. The punch, coming from Lanny, seemed less a gesture of violence than a reach for a star.

"Elvis gives people hope," he said. He then told me about a family reunion where he had sung "Are You Lonesome To-night?" to his grandmother, a moment so heaped with emotion that many of his relatives had to step from the room to wipe away a tear. Lanny Boy paused a moment and gazed up into the rafters. He sang a line or two for me, and the truth is it wasn't bad. The rendering for his grandmother, he admitted, had even brought a tear to his own eye.

"Right here," Lanny said, and pointed to a fleck of sawdust on his cheek.

In my last months at the mill, as I wondered what sort of behavior the unrequited nature of Whiskey-Tim's love for Cheri would manifest, Lanny Boy bore a wrinkle in his own happy demeanor. After six years at the mill, he was fed up with being thought a spy by the younger workers and wore the reputation with about as much patience as he did a canker sore. Had he been born a hundred years earlier, Lanny might have been a teamster and worked in a setting with creatures more amicable to his good nature. He was nearly as big as a horse himself, and I believe a horse would have swooned on hearing his soothing whisper. A horse, also a sensitive being, would have immediately sensed Lanny's gentleness and would have responded favorably to his friendly coaxing. Out in the deep woods with these noble and useful animals and a sleigh laden with logs, Lanny would have avoided the mill crew and could have been himself without giving offense.

The trouble was he had not only hitched himself in the barbed wire of the younger workers' opinion, but he'd also alienated the older workers by smoking marijuana in Red Eye's van during lunch breaks. The older crewmen already thought the younger workers were disrespectful, spiteful, and lazy, and these mealtime joyrides proved it beyond doubt. Every day Randy and I would watch the spectacle from the Blazer. The drug buddies, as we sardonically referred to them, would pile into the upholstered back end of the van and peel off for town. Twenty minutes later the van would come roaring back down Bacon Street and whip into the parking lot, where the side door would open, emitting a puff of blue smoke in the shape of a mini-mushroom cloud. Behind the cloud, giggling for all they were worth, stumbled the drug buddies. And it was true that Lanny Boy was often among them. Emerging from the smoke, he made himself more conspicuous by trying to affect an air of innocence. Such a compromising position ended whatever honeymoon Lanny was on with the older workers.

Randy and I saw the fallout the one and only time we took our lunch in the break room. A little past noon on that day, Lanny wandered in, dropped a couple of coins in the rattling old Coke machine, lifted his soda pop from the slot, and took a seat at one of the picnic tables. These ancient tables, frayed and sagging, were painted forest green as if to cover the mold of old conversation. Lanny had lit up and smoked half a cigarette before he noticed the silence. Just before he came in, a half dozen of the older men—Gus, Del, Henry, Lee, and a couple of others—had been sitting

around having a lively talk about the weather, hunting, and
John Deere tractors.

"Why's everyone so quiet?" Lanny asked.

"Why aren't you out with your friends?" someone asked
in return.

"Because I'm in here," Lanny said.

"Aren't your friends going to miss you?"

"No."

"Who's going to pay for the wacky-tabacky today, then?"

"How would I know?"

"Because you do it, too."

"Not necessarily."

"See, he can't answer us a straight no."

"I should be able to come in here without being hassled."

"Where's that written?"

"It's a public break room."

"It's not public. It's private."

"You know what I mean."

"Smokin' that stuff, you can't think straight."

"I think fine."

"I'll bet it's worse than wacky-tabacky out there, too."

"How would you know?"

"You think we don't know? Think again."

"I don't know what you think."

"Why don't you go back to your friends? Go on."

When Lanny was near tears, the grilling stopped. There
was a wounded feeling among the older men that Lanny had
betrayed them, that he had slipped out from under their
wing and turned immediately to set fire to their feathers.

For five years Lanny had felt privileged in two realms

within the mill and then in a wink discovered he was an out-
sider in both. He was considered a spy in one camp, a drug
buddy in the other, when all those years what he thought
he had been was a confidant and a good sport. In his own
mind, he was a good man who had been slandered by those
he considered family. Out in the mill, when he thought too
long about the injustice of it all, he would slam things. He
would pick up big oak cants, slam them onto the stack, and
then stand hulked and panting, staring down at the wood
as if daring it to fight back. Between boards and cants, he
swore. Gentle as he was, he knew all the big words. He'd blow
his big smoke rings and thrust his fist through them with the
smooth flinch of a boxer, but again, because it was Lanny,
you dismissed the anger as no more than a tantrum, a dust
tornado about to die out in a pile of dry leaves.

But that spring I underestimated his hurt. I assumed
his easygoing nature, the gleam of trust he presented to the
world, could withstand a practical joke. I was wrong. Even
during the planning stages, I sensed that I was about to put
wings on a wood tick, but I kept going anyway.

In those days there was a well-known boxer who shared
a last name with Randy and me. Mickey Goodwin was a
middleweight who fought out of the Kronk Gym in Detroit
and was considered a future champion. Lanny loved boxing
almost as much as disco music, so it wasn't hard to raise his
brow when I told him Mickey, or the Mickster, as I called
him, was my cousin. The first thing Lanny Boy said was
"You're lying," to which I should have answered "You're
right" and ended it there. But I was appalled that Lanny
would know I had lied to him, so I kept going.

I shoveled it for all it was worth. It lifted easier than sawdust, spilled golden over the edges, and, though I knew it
was only fool's gold, it was perfect mulch for a story. I told
Lanny I was Mickey's favorite cousin and that as boys we
had spent summer vacations together, swimming, playing
basketball, going to the movies, and eating pizza. Of course,
the Mickster had to watch his weight, so out of considera-
tion for his future success I was obliged to eat most of the
pizza. Lanny's mouth dropped as he listened. I could see that
I was convincing, that I should have stopped there, but I
kept going.

I told him my mother and Mickey's mother were sisters
and that was how we were related. This gust of blighted sawdust was barely off my tongue when I realized it meant both
sisters would have had to marry men with the same last
name. As I stood staring up into Lanny's face, hoping silence
would equal composure, I wondered when he'd figure it out
and I'd have to confess. But the rings of a family tree weren't
things to which Lanny gave a lot of thought, and the board
slipped through without leaving a sliver. I really should have
stopped there, but again I kept going.

Cousin Mickey was often in the sports pages. Wouldn't it
be something, I thought, to have a newspaper article about
the Mickster with the Mickster's autograph next to it? When
I ran this idea past Randy, he said enough was enough, that
the game was up and it was time to see it. I pleaded with him
to scratch me a forgery but he wouldn't, so I convinced his
wife to do it instead. She gave me an "I'll do it if you'll go
away" look and signed Mickey's name to the paper. Her cur-
sive was a little fancy, but the thing sufficed.

When Lanny Boy saw it, all he could do was nod his innocent head and say "Wow." When I told him he could take
the paper home, he gloated. It wasn't Elvis paraphernalia,
but it was pretty good stuff nonetheless. The dreamy glint,
nearly extinguished by the spy business, returned to Lanny's
eye. I felt I'd done a good deed.

But that same Friday, somewhere on the road home, that
winged tick finally found the target it had been destined for
since the beginning. It flew in and bit me squarely on the
arse, which, apparently, is where my conscience was located
in those days. The guilt swelled such that I could barely sit
with myself. I knew there was only one thing to do.

All weekend I fretted about the confession. I imagined
Lanny in a stiff black-and-white collar, nodding his head, his
gentle voice cracked with pain, reminding me that I'd had
several opportunities to repent, but I'd kept going. Come
Monday it was almost that bad. The shadows off the machinery were longer, more gothic than usual, and the blackbirds on the rafters had the hunched readiness of vultures
about to pluck heartily from the meaty flanks of my shame.

After I admitted the scam, Lanny took the cigarette from
his mouth and straightened. He looked at me with dull eyes
but also with a quietness that was piercing. When he got his
bearings, he called me a name and walked away.

I told him I was sorry, which took some of the red from
the bite on my conscience but didn't help much overall. A
month passed before Lanny even began to forgive me. He
spoke to me only once during that time. He was passing by
the big entrance and called in to me, "You still think you're
funny?"

I shrugged and looked away. I stared down into the popple cant I was about to stack as if there, in the pale grain, was a road map out. Out of what, I wasn't sure. Out of my troubles, my mistakes. Maybe I was looking for a way out of myself. I thought if I looked hard enough, long enough, I'd see one. But I learned that recognition of a way out comes slowly, by degrees, because slowly it got better with Lanny and then it was fixed. I don't know how it got fixed; it's a mystery. All I know is that before the weather turned hot we were back to talking about disco and boxing and the king of rock and roll.

BOB TALE

WHENEVER I RECALL Bob the maintenance man—
he of the blue coveralls—I am thankful he is
blessedly intact and that I didn't kill him the night of the
Christmas party. I'm further grateful that bouncing him off
the roof of the Blazer didn't lobotomize the good nature
right out of him.

Bob was fifty-two or fifty-three years old, but at the end
of a long, hot day, when he angled across the yard with his
shirt off, you would have sworn he was twenty-seven, which
is what good posture and no belly to speak of will do for you.
I'd wince when I saw him coming, knowing time wasn't
likely to chisel me up as well as it had Bob.

On days when the saws were down, Bob would sometimes ask me to help with a fix-it project. While Bob gutted
and reglued the mill's weary machinery, my part was usually
nothing more than to gofer tools back and forth from the
tool room, but occasionally the work had an element of adventure to it. The time we fixed the floor cleaner is a good
example.

The floor cleaner extended out a hole in the wall at the
south end of the mill and rose up like an escalator over the

sawdust pit (in effect giving my grounded freighter a bow-sprit). A chain with rungs revolved around the shaft, the rungs nudging the sawdust up from a concrete trench inside the mill to the summit, where either the wind blew it off into the fields east of the mill or it drizzled into the pit below. Before long, of course, the pit would fill up and become a small mountain. When Bob told me we had to fix the little engine at the end of the floor cleaner, I hoped all that was required was a leisurely stroll up the slope. But Lightning Joe, operating the front-end loader, had recently converted twenty feet of mountain into twenty feet of pit, which meant twenty feet of open air to fall through.

As we crawled out the hole in the wall onto the narrow ledge between the building and the pit, tools in tow, I looked down and said, "Wow." Actually, I used a different word but *wow* will suffice. In response Bob said that if we were to fall off the floor cleaner (which was barely two feet wide) it might not kill us but it would sure hurt. I knew we were working nowhere near the windswept elevations of, say, those brave iron and cable workers who had built the Mackinac Bridge, but the old joke *it's not the fall but the sudden stop* was still relevant.

Anyway, we started up. Bob went first. I was thinking that if I were his age a glance down would have killed me, but there was Bob going up like a caterpillar on a twig. He was slow but fearless. I was right behind him with three sizes of crescent wrench in one hand and a death grip on the floor cleaner with the other. Wow.

"Grab my ankles if I fall," Bob called back when we were at the top. We were flat on our stomachs on the cleaner, and

I was looking up at the bottom of his boots (I think Bob secretly liked this, a young whippersnapper like me having to sniff his heels). I could even see the little tag that read "oil resistant." I thought it unlikely that I'd be able to grab Bob's ankles while gripping those three crescent wrenches in one hand and saving my own neck with the other, but I thought I'd explore the question anyway in case I was able to manage it.

"How long could you hang upside down before your head exploded?" I inquired. Maybe it was the wind out there on the peak, but I thought I heard Bob laugh.

He then began to call for the crescent wrenches by saying big, medium, or small, and I handed them up accordingly. Everything was done more or less by touch. Bob would put his hand back and I'd lay the instrument in his palm with the firm care of a surgeon's nurse. Every few seconds I dared a peek down, and there was the sawdust pit, looming like the top of a volcano. The view made me dizzy, but I was already lying flat so I figured I was half safe, which was better than nothing. While I lay there in a slightly nauseous funk, Bob performed his magic and the thing was done. After we climbed down, my legs shook for an hour, but I was fine. Though only meager tool boy, I thought I'd contributed mightily. Meanwhile, Bob went cheerfully to his next project, which, he told me with a shrug, had something to do with bare wires and electricity.

THE ROOKIE

THE ROOKIE WAS a short, potbellied nineteen-year-old whose head was as wide as his shoulders. Because of his build I tried to nickname him "the Worm," but it never stuck. The Rookie was always the Rookie even after he was no longer the new man.

The Rookie had ventured to the sawmill to become hardened. I'd come for a little starching myself, but the Rookie was much more conspicuous about it. He voiced early on that he was at the mill to become hardened, thereby making his lessons much—there is only one word for it—*harder* than they needed to be. He learned, for instance, that it was one thing to become hardened and a different thing entirely to be accepted as hardened. The latter is a problem of perception, which meant the Rookie was up against it. With the posture of a question mark and the muscle tone of a marshmallow, the Rookie was hardly more intimidating than a dandelion. And there was no redemption in his wide face, which was set with an opacity that seemed to filter out nonsense and take only facts into account; to the stacking crew, the Rookie's whole demeanor suspiciously resembled arrogance.

A century ago, the Rookie would have been an office boy (an uppity one surely), running errands and doing minor accounting work in leather-bound ledger books for companies that cut the big pine. He would have worn breeches and a stiff collar and, because of his asthma and frail build, would have felt unsure of himself out in the open. With much the same to overcome in his actual life, he'd have needed a solid decade, probably longer, to be considered hardened, and even then it was no sure thing.

In part the Rookie was a victim of the mill's shorthand, which was in place mostly because of the noise. The noise in a sawmill is staggering. It's like the sudden appearance of a freighter in a trout stream, overwhelming to the point of disbelief. The roar of the mill would begin in the machinery—all of which seemed to have a terrible case of whooping cough—rumble across the floor, crash into the aluminum walls, bounce off and gather at the center of the big room, and plume upward to the rafters, where it would ruffle the feathers of the blackbirds before it trickled back to the floor in the form of sawdust. This is not a scientific description of noise, of course, but just the way it seemed.

Once adapted you could use this thick curtain of sound for your own purposes. You could clam up and be sullen and nobody would know the difference, you could sing loudly and badly at the top of your lungs (which I often did) and no one would care, or you could act as though you couldn't hear a thing and people would leave you to your own devices. The noise was an indomitable, immovable, invisible, and often convenient wall. The only drawback was a bit of audio schizophrenia. Your ears retreated from the noise and then lurched eagerly forth to catch the briefest snatch of conversation. In other words, the noise made your eardrums do sit-ups.

Because of the noise two types of shorthand developed in the mill. One was sign language, which included the oft-used gesture of positioning your fists side by side, as if gripping an imaginary stick, and then snapping your wrists downward to indicate "break time." There was drawing your finger across your throat to mean "stop"; a circular motion with your finger, which meant "keep it going" or "start it up" or "the SOB is crazy!"; and the deep, exaggerated shrug of the shoulders that could mean anything from "I'm lost" to "Who the hell knows?"

Nicknames were a kind of shorthand, too, and because the noise didn't allow a lengthy verbal analysis of one another's character, a nickname had to carry most of the burden of description. Hence, to be tagged a rookie at the mill meant that in the considered opinion of your coworkers you didn't know a board from a sawdust pile or a banana from a buzz saw. It meant that you were naive, witless, and, at least until you proved otherwise, a wimp. The Rookie had troubles beyond this. He was prone to using three- and four-syllable words and, worse, spoke them precisely if not to say exquisitely. Worse yet, he knew what they meant. Big words at a sawmill are not generally reckoned to be good things. They put your average mill hand on guard mentally when he needs all his resources to be on guard physically. A mill hand will know that big, complicated words are being spoken at him no matter how damned noisy it is, and in his mind the speaker will evolve quickly into an object of suspicion. And, as the Rookie's case proved, once you have fallen under suspicion at the mill being recognized as hardened (or authorized) is a long shot at best.

But despite the obvious contempt of his workmates, the Rookie kept heaping it on himself. He admitted, for instance, that it was his wife's idea that he come to the mill for the toughening. This was plainly admitting you were a wimp, although, in the Rookie's case, the only real fallout was that we all secretly wanted a glance at this woman who had such a precise notion of her future and the man in it. We never got a look at this mystical personage, but we witnessed at least the partial success of her project, for the Rookie did score some toughening points.

For one thing he picked up some swear words, which he mixed with his big words (although he was too careful to sound out each syllable, the truth being that his voice was too opulent for the quick-strike effect swearing required). For another he left his jacket home most mornings, braving the spring chill in his T-shirt and rubbing the goose bumps on his arms with admirable discretion. This newfound fettle gave him the spine to tell a man in the bar eyeballing his wife to take a hike, a request that was complied with. We were skeptical of this self-reported triumph until the day we saw the Rookie willing to take his boldness to the point of disaster. That morning, fed up with taking orders from the Cat (who always chased him off to stack boards, lighter but brisker work than stacking cants), he stood his ground and refused. When the Cat threatened him with a whipping, the

Rookie folded his arms, drew us in with a deliberate set of his head, and said, "My, you have a lot of confidence."

There was a sudden silence. Every speck of sawdust swirling in the air, eighty-nine billion of them, stopped to see what would happen next. We humans waited, too, our breath harbored around our tonsils. David looked up at his Goliath, a small, and I think praying, smile on his lips. Maybe he considered a swat from the Cat the final exam of his hardening-school career, but the Cat wasn't a Philistine and all he did was laugh. The laughter echoed, and the Rookie, more discouraged than relieved, turned and headed for the boards. I believe he thought he had failed, but I think he passed the test of nerves, grandly. He was still able to walk. There had been no blood. I would have given him a B+.

But, as I say, the Rookie was up against it. The blow that took him down, ironically, was verbal. One afternoon, Gus, the grizzled but gentle old cuss who operated the gang saw, walked up to the Rookie and, in a tone drenched with impatience for the entire charade, said, "You don't belong in a sawmill. You belong in a flower shop." Another speck stopper. Gus waited while his words resonated, saw they wouldn't need repeating, and walked away. I stood nearby and watched a gallon of fortitude drain from the Rookie's face. He made a little smile out of the ruins and shook his head. I thought I heard a peep, maybe the beginning of a cry, but he got a hold on it, performed some mental technique on it, and stacked it away. For this I would have given him an A+.

A week after Gus's dig the Rookie left the mill. From him I learned that honesty about your agenda is a hard thing, and

I admired him for it, though maybe for his heart more than his common sense. In the end we knew the Rookie, in his convoluted way, was still out there searching. The last we heard he'd entered his wife in a wet T-shirt contest.

STIG

STIG HOVERS in my memory with a scoop shovel beneath his arm. He was sixty-two years old, a tall, lurching figure of iron physical strength but with a face as soft as bread pudding. Stig was the mill's cleanup man, and decked out in his denim overcoat, overalls, stocking cap, and rubber boots he looked like what I imagined must be the prototype version of an American peasant. It was a look I also assigned to myself, although I lacked the contentment I knew Stig must feel with every breath he took.

For Stig seemed a titan of simplicity. Everything about his life seemed pared down to the essentials, everything a basic, comforting shade of gray. He drove a little gray pickup, lived in a tiny gray trailer along Route 55, and came and went from the sawmill as he pleased. Inside the fence he carried his short-handled scoop shovel everywhere and moved in the same slow clop from one job to the next, as regular as a change in the Michigan weather. The one exception to this mundane ethos was the mittens. He wore big leather mittens dyed the color of a yield sign. Against the snowy landscape of the yard, these yellow monsters almost

made you wince. Had they been Coast Guard strobe lights, the mittens would have lit up half of Lake Huron.

One icy February morning, fingers brittle with cold, I found myself eyeballing Stig's mittens with a kind of hunger. Intrinsic in the mittens was the message that you couldn't really stack the heavy cants with such cumbersome hand warmers, so, in order to enjoy their comfort, you would have to find work more compatible with their fit, work less exposed to the elements. Life, the mitten message said, was about finding lighter wood to tote and better insulation. Among the stackers the mittens were a kind of goal, and they elevated Stig to the status of a philosopher.

In the truck at break time, I told Randy that with his big yellow mittens Stig was the great gray guru of contentment and confessed that there were moments when Whiskey-Tim and I would have traded places with him in an instant. Wanting to suddenly chop forty years off the end of our lives couldn't have reflected well on our state of mind, but the weariness that got into your bones from the heavy stacking often made its way to your head, too.

Randy listened until I finished and then lifted an eyebrow and cocked his head with a little shrug of irony. He was quiet for a moment and then said:

"Get a look at his hand."

"His hand?"

"His right hand."

"Why?"

"Just do it."

"Why?"

"You'll see."

I tried to get him to tell me about Stig's right hand, but he sat stubbornly silent, implying it was something I needed to see for myself in order to get the full drift.

So after lunch, my curiosity piqued, I snuck down to the north end where Stig was sending two-by-fours through the notcher, a screeching, tablelike machine that grooved the wood into runners for the pallets. As I moved between the stacks of boards, hoping for a glimpse, Stig slipped the mitten from his right hand to steal a pinch from his can of Copenhagen. Old Stig had probably been dipping for fifty-two of his sixty-two years and performed the move so adroitly that his hand was back in the mitten before I could get a good look. I returned to the green chains, thinking the only way I was going to see that hand was to pull off the mitten myself.

I was back to the drudgery, stacking a big oak cant, when an idea seemed to leap out of the sawdust and stand saluting before me. It occurred to me that Stig rarely spoke a word and responded to nearly all overtures with a wave. I had heard him utter a few timid sentences but had seen him wave a hundred times.

A half hour later I was back at the north end, pretending to count pallet stock. As I peeked around a stack of runners, Stig suddenly whipped off the glove and brought out the Copenhagen; at that very moment, I waved to him. Without hesitation Stig waved back, and I got a good zoom on his bare right hand. Gone were two fingers, part of a third, and almost his entire thumb. His hand had been mutilated.

"What happened?" I asked Randy in the truck at the afternoon break.

"Rumor is he stuck his hand in the notcher on purpose."

The notcher blades, as ferocious as the fangs of a rabid wolf, had done a number on the great philosopher's hand. Randy told me Stig had hoped to get a monthly permanent disability check and retire early, but in the ensuing court battle an agreement was reached that the mill management would offer him work he could do with one arm (operating the notcher was one of the jobs!) and he would continue to be employed.

I was knocked out of my holey socks to learn this about Stig. Suddenly the gray in his life wasn't the soothing color of the mundane but the scudding aftermath of a terrible storm. The one small, bright light in the story was that the manager had gone out and plucked Stig's fingers from the sawdust, sealed them in a plastic bag, and driven them to the hospital in Cadillac to be reattached. The fingers couldn't be saved, but the noble attempt somehow tapered the sadness of the whole affair.

Stig's story taught me that I might be susceptible to interpreting someone's numbness as contentment; thus, I became more cynical, but more careful, afterward. And I decided my hands weren't nearly so cold after all.

Eventually I figured out that leather gloves, no matter how well stitched and pricey, didn't stand a chance against rough-hewn oak. A pair cost a good percentage of my paycheck (money I preferred to spend on junk food) and were not nearly the value of the cheap white pair with the small black beads on the palms and fingers that I could buy for less than two dollars at the party store. The plastic beads held up much better against the scathing friction of the wood, and a pair would last a fortnight or better. To have figured out the cost-benefit of these gloves was a triumph and proved I could figure out something besides how to feel sorry for myself. All, in a sad way, thanks to Stig.

THE RUG

THESE DAYS it's not only old photographs that remind me of the sawmill. A pulp truck rattling my side-view mirror with a whoosh out on Old U.S. 27, a heap of discarded pallets at a construction site, or a tree no longer attached to its roots will send up the image of the mill. Anyone wearing a cast, brace, or bandage, or simply walking with a limp, will cause me to wince in recognition. For some reason, I keep five acorns on top of my bookshelf and a sprinkle of needles from a tall red pine on my worktable, and they, too, remind me of the sawmill. Flannel shirts, coveralls, and hard hats, the more tattered the better, all speak, if not sing, the language of the mill. Then there's the rug.

Technically, it's not really a rug. A narrow piece of carpeting stretching from the front door to the kitchen table is what my beloved calls a runner, although—start the music here—it looks like a rug to me. It's embroidered with five distinct leaf patterns, one of which is supposed to be a maple leaf, but with the leaflets of its blade overly round it could easily represent a hand that's been run over by a skidder. A cartoonish rug, then, but it, too, reminds me of the mill.

Sometimes this rug, or runner, gets out of line and needs to be pulled forward. And when I'm bent over, giving it a little tug, I realize that in the act there is a metaphor about history, about why people avoid history and claim to hate it as if it's a moldy biscuit being shoved down their throats. I don't think of history in this way, but I can understand why so many do. I can understand why reaching back to pull forward any part of history can cause revulsion. For, to state it obviously, to consider history is to see human beings behaving at less than their best.

The human beings who populate the history of logging—the little corner of the world I've decided is a part of me and me of it—these humans, many of them, behaved atrociously. They are guilty of raping the forests, polluting the rivers, crushing the morale of men, and destroying the public trust. The cutover, as the stripping of the forest came to be known, gave false hope to farmers, who found the only seeds the barren land could sustain were those of pine and hardwood trees, a harvest too distant for anyone but the truest forester to contemplate. A diet of avarice, arrogance, and a few million ravaged acres, anyone? I have sympathy for those who find this wearisome, revolting, or even dull. Why look at history when all you can feel is disgust?

One answer, also obvious, is that, although it has grave limitations, history is our best guide to the future. Another answer, again obvious, is that history has many sides. The human beings who populate the history of logging often behaved well, too, many of them the very beings who behaved so poorly. They are guilty of creating jobs by the tens of thousands; funding hospitals, libraries, and schools; building roads and railways; and, not least, supplying the material to put roofs over the heads of an entire civilization. Some of them even replanted the trees.

I can see both sides of the coin. I can talk out of both sides of my mouth. This brings me back to the rug and the metaphor. The rug is history and on it stands good things and bad, and when I stand on the rug myself I know how hard it is to pull it in any direction much less the right one. And it's nearly impossible to pull forward only the part with the maple leaf, the part, in other words, that represents the sweet taste. The point of all this, without forgetting all that was bad and wasteful and evil, is that it's not entirely impossible either. You can pull the sweet spot forward, you can pull forward history worthy of your attention, and you can pull forward that which will enrich your life if you're willing to see the openings.

The next few paragraphs, I hope, are anecdotal evidence that openings exist.

I remember how long ago my grandfather would drive me and my younger brothers, Rory and Rob, down a winding road of sand and gravel to the banks of the backwaters of the Reedsburg Dam and a boat livery called Rube's. Rube owned a big Labrador retriever named Duke, locally famous for drinking beer and eating cigarette butts, and while Grandpa arranged for the boat my brothers and I would pet old Duke's head, wishing we were old enough to share vices with this worldly critter. After Rube had fobbed off all my grandfather's attempts to pay for the boat, we'd pile in, three young boys in life jackets, fishing poles and tackle box in tow, shoving off with our sixty-three-year-old grandfather, who pulled the oars through the dark, weedy water until we were out past the point some seventy yards from shore, out there "in the boondocks" as we used to quip, until some combination of instinct and experience would tell Grandpa to stop rowing and say, "This is a good spot."

He would then toss a concrete anchor shaped like a moonshine jug over the side of the boat and help us bait our hooks with the night crawlers we had dug up near the mulch pile in Grandma's garden. Settled in, we would fish for perch, bluegills, and sunfish, unaware that a bluegill is a sunfish, not that it mattered. We were out on the water with fishing poles and Grandpa. That was all that mattered.

We would fish for an hour, catch seven or eight keepers, and throw three or four shorties back. We would drink root beer and eat Hershey bars with one hand and grip our poles with the other. Grandpa would smoke a cigarette or two and scan the shoreline for deer and the skyline for rain. We would watch the bugs skitter along the onyx surface of the floodwater and daydream. I'd daydream about baseball, Batman, jet fighter planes, and, with what must have been a Freudian twitch, being pushed around in a shopping cart by beautiful women. My brothers, too, would be off in a la-la land of their own. When there wasn't a fish to be caught and the silence and stillness had gone on long enough, Grandpa would say, "We'd better get back."

But on one trip we didn't go directly back, and I don't recall that we ever went directly back again. Instead, Grandpa aimed the boat for shore fifty yards down from the livery. The closer we got to land the more the water cleared and the more Grandpa eased his rowing so he could look over the side. When we had drifted to a stop, we saw what he was searching for. There, in the lighted water about four feet down, lay squares of cedar in rows, as neatly toppled as dominoes.

"Those are shingles," Grandpa said. "We're sitting over an old shingle mill." He then told us about Michelson, the old lumber town mentioned earlier and now under the backwaters of the Reedsburg Dam. It had once been home to five hundred people whose lives seemed to us as obscure as the shadowy banks across the floodplain. Grandpa explained the business about the flood, how it had been caused on purpose, and was mildly amused at our shock that five hundred people would be allowed to drown when someone must have known the flood was coming.

"Nobody drowned," he said finally, leaving it to our boy logic to figure out the details, the logistics, of how disaster had been avoided. He didn't have time to explain for he was too entranced. Sitting over the shingle mill, a small, mysterious smile appeared on his lips. The heat, the swirl of insects, the breeze flipping the narrow leaves of the willow trees up on shore seemed to have put him in another realm altogether. For a few moments you really couldn't talk to Grandpa. This was the mystery, the mysterious thing, for Grandpa was almost always accessible. For five full minutes we sat as quietly as three boys in a small space have ever been, observing our grandfather, who seemed to have waded out to some depth beyond words. And then, in the time it takes to savor a square of chocolate and as quietly as the afternoon shade stretches east, he came back.

"Let's go home," he said, and he pointed the bow of the boat toward Rube's, where old Duke waited to eat fish.

I have thought about that mysterious smile of Grandpa's for years. He was a quiet man, and in the years since his death, as I've matured and reflected, I've decided he was somewhat of a brooding man, too. But there was nothing of the brood in that smile during those gorgeous moments on the still water over the shingle mill at Michelson. In that smile was satisfaction, contentment, and something approaching peace with the world. The mystery of that smile was in the literal fathom between the bottom of the boat and the top of the shingle mill.

My father told me that as a young man my grandpa often hopped a train in Merritt—this would have been the Grand Rapids and Indiana Railroad from Cadillac—and rode it out to Michelson on Friday nights. On Friday nights Michelson was the place to be. There was dancing, drinking, card games, horseshoe pitching, and storytelling. There were a dozen more things besides, and, of course, there was youth to account for the gleam in Grandpa's eye. I think there was even more to it than that.

It was likely, there in the boat, that Grandpa was thinking of the whole landscape of northern Michigan in 1924. He wasn't just above the shingle mill. He was on the train, riding through fields he'd helped farm; he was fording rivers he'd fished and from which he'd cut ice; and he was walking through woods he'd once hunted. He was thinking of the thrill of arriving in Michelson with its population of a few hundred, a virtual metropolis compared to Merritt with its meager few dozen. He would have liked spending time in a town still largely moved by steam and horsepower where the cards were dealt onto an upturned nail keg in the light of a lantern or a candle smushed into a sardine tin.

He would have liked the way the voices rose and fell like dust in the road, real voices, not the monotone imitations that come through wires and cables but true voices that you could find just by walking down the road to the boarding-house or the next barn, voices that, combined with the quivering catgut of a violin, made the sweetest music you had ever heard.

He would have liked that somebody, one of the old-timers probably, would have known the numbers, that this old boy, in his suspenders and work boots, his flannel shirt battened down at the wrists and collar (even though it was eighty degrees in the dusky shade), would have known how many board feet had been cut that week, how many shingles were produced, and how many flatcars had been marked, loaded, and sent to market.

My grandpa would have liked that even on a Saturday night prudence was sprinkled about in abundance, that it seemed to fall from above like droplets from a rain-soaked oak, and that this particular brand of prudence wasn't afraid to knock a couple of heads together if the drinking got more important than the card game or the horseshoe pitching.

My grandfather would have been of the philosophy that men had the right to reshape the forest responsibly and would have agreed with the notion that the forest shaped back, that a flesh and blood man became as much a product of the forest as a tree became a plank or a piece of paper.

Of course, I'm only guessing what my grandfather's thoughts were. I can only glean from his smile, which was mysterious but also seemed to be cresting toward joy. In the end I don't know what he was thinking or why he was smiling, but I know it doesn't matter that much. It's enough to know that Grandpa was pulling forward the part of the rug with the maple leaf.

LIGHTNING

He WAS never mentioned once. Not in the sawmill, not in the parking lot, and not in the break room, where the cigarette smoke formed a blue swirl around the florescent light and the older men of the crew sat with one eye on the clock and sipped coffee and talked a million words about news, weather, and sports but never one about him. My conclusion is that television and radio had obliterated him off a mill worker's (and everyone else's) mental map, a sociological observation about as original as a pail of sawdust but probably the truth of the matter. Nothing at all reminded me of him, not brawny men in flannel shirts on packages of paper towels, not the big steers in the pastures around Merritt, and not the log piles or sawdust mountains south of the mill. He was dead. He had been dead for a long time. It was sad in a way.

The last tale I remember hearing about Paul Bunyan was in the mid-1960s when I was seven years old. Randy had told me that the Great Lakes, the Mississippi River, and the Grand Canyon were formed by big Paul dragging his big ax along the ground. It's likely this story was also in a picture book because I have a pretty clear memory of Paul in his flannel shirt, his massive shoulders drooped, dragging his ax as if he were a Little Leaguer dragging his bat back to the bench after striking out. Why Paul was in such a sad state I don't recall. He'd lost a girl maybe or Babe the blue ox had passed on or maybe he was just bored. I believed the story up until about the age of nine, not only believed it but cherished it and even cherished it after I'd stopped believing it. It saddened me to learn that our natural wonders were the result of volcanic activity, glacial pullback, and erosion rather than raw human emotion. I much preferred the Paul Bunyan version and wanted it to be true. But then, as I say, I was nine.

A handsome man despite teeth as wide as a mule's, Lightning Joe was a man of legend in his own right with his own oxen sidekick, albeit a mechanical one. Joe drove the Grabber, the big tractor with the big clamp that held the logs aloft like scrolls in a fist and hauled them from the log field to the peeler deck. Because of its odd, prehistoric look, you never forgot the Grabber. Because of tales tall enough to have been written on the scrolls, you never forgot its driver. In terms of satisfying your hunger for whoppers, Lightning Joe made Paul Bunyan obsolete.

I remember two stories from Joe, the first being the lightning story. One morning, as we walked back to the mill after break time, Randy nudged me into asking Joe if he thought a storm was brewing. Randy had informed me of Joe's claim to have been hit by lightning no less than a dozen times, and, looking up into the nearly cloudless sky of a late summer afternoon, I thought the only thing in the forecast was a practical joke but decided I'd play along. I quickened my step, and in the dusty strip of ground between the log field and the break room I caught up with Joe and asked if he thought a storm was festering.

"Well, if it is," Joe said, wincing upward, "you don't want to be around me."

"Why not?" I asked.

"I've been hit by lightning a dozen times, seven of them right here in the mill yard."

I gave Randy a glance and then looked back at Joe.

"It's my body chemistry," Joe said with a straight face. "I attract electricity."

I looked back at Randy, then again at Joe, awaiting the cloudburst of laughter. But Randy's expression remained stoic, and Lightning Joe's was straight as ever. It was no put-on.

"I'm lucky to be alive," Joe said.

Back to stacking boards, I waited for one of them to come along and deliver the punch line, waited, in other words, for lightning to strike, but it never did.

Later, in autumn, Randy goaded me into asking Joe why he hunted deer with a pistol.

"He hunts deer with a pistol? Is that legal?"

"Ask him."

Walking into the break room one afternoon, I told Joe I'd heard a rumor he hunted whitetail with a pistol. Joe halted in his tracks. His expression turned grave as he nodded with all the solemnity of the accursed.

"I have to," he said. "It makes it easier when they charge you."

Apparently, Lightning Joe was often attacked by herds of deer. That very season a buck and two does had charged his deer blind, galloping across the meadow so fast, Joe said with a straight face, that there was no time to lift his rifle to shoot. All he could do was hit the ground, roll over, pull out his pistol, and fire several twisting shots as the deer leaped over his blind. The two doe he felled with gut shots; the buck, naturally, he felled with a shot through the heart.

"Now I never go into the woods without a pistol," Joe said.

So ended the deer story.

A century ago Joe would have been in charge of unloading the logs from the trains that chugged into the mill yard. To do his work he would have used a boom and thick ropes and all manner of physics, all of it combined to form a wheelless ancestor of the Grabber. Under the lustrous blue skies of 1890, Joe, a loyal company man in any era, would have unloaded the logs with efficiency and enthusiasm, and, with the gravity of a man in danger, he would have told his stories. No saying what he might have regaled the crew with a hundred years ago. Perhaps he'd have cleared the area of wolf and wolverine with hardly more than a big stick and a derringer or tackled a bear with no more than a penknife. He might even have sucked a tornado or two into his lungs and blown out a summer breeze, all of this, of course, when he wasn't dodging lightning.

For a time I thought Joe was taking me for a fool with his tall tales, but then it hit me that this was about something other than my glut of gullibility. While it was true that after listening to Joe's stories I felt I needed waders that would tie up at least as high as my neck, the more I thought about it the more I wondered why that should be a big deal.

Didn't I, too, want to shade the truth about my life and my sawmill experience in particular? Indeed, I wanted to tell friends and family that stacking lumber was a skilled occupation and management spent good money scouting out just the right people to do it. I wanted to boast to everyone that I been recruited, tested, and certified and had earned the equivalent in lumber stacking to a black belt in karate. I wanted to tell the world I was being considered for the Green Chain Hall of Fame and that someday a plaque with my bronzed mug would be hung on the wall in the neat, well-kept logging museum at the Hartwick Pines State Park in Grayling. I wanted, in short, for people to know I was alive and vital.

It was through Joe telling his big stories that I realized if I were ever to find maturity in this raucous sawdust pile I'd have to accept that there were winking aspects to everyone's personality, mental nodes of self-deception that simply allowed one to swing out of bed in the morning. The oddity of most people, I was learning, was nothing more than an innocent attempt to say "Here I am."

Somehow it all became clear when Randy told me that Joe liked to dress like a cowboy on Friday night—hat, chaps, spurs, and enough turquoise jewelry to choke a tourist—and make the rounds of the local bars. Hearing this, I asked myself what was the harm, even if it meant believing your own tall tales, of giving your life a little pizzazz now and then? Lightning and deer make the meadows and woods intriguing after all. And leave it to Lightning Joe to show that one way to buck the boredom was to dress like Pecos Bill.

OUTSIDE THE FENCE

IN THOSE MONTHS at the sawmill, the outside world seemed no larger than a wood chip, although that didn't prevent the crew's collective commentary on it. In the break room, opinion about current events hung as thick as the cigarette smoke. To wit, the hostages in Iran came home because the Iranians were afraid that President Reagan, more ruthless than President Carter, would bomb the hell out of them. The American hockey team beat the Soviet hockey team because democracy beats the hell out of communism any day. John Lennon was killed because the world is full of lunatics, and Reagan, a few months later, was damn near killed for the same reason.

In those months we ridiculed an old man who had died because he wouldn't leave an exploding Mount Saint Helens, ridiculed him as if we weren't stubborn ourselves. A freighter slammed into the Sunshine Skyway Bridge in Florida, killing thirty-five people, and we thought what a way to go and God be with them.

In those months Bjorn Borg won Wimbledon again because he had that fragile and endangered thing called a work ethic, the Steelers dropped the curtain on the Rams for yet another Super Bowl victory, and the Phillies won the World Series because the odds were finally with the City of Brotherly Love.

Across the big pond in those days, Charles and Di married and made a happy balcony appearance, God bless them; and Pope John Paul II took two bullets and forgave the gunman, God bless him. In Yugoslavia, Marshall Tito died— another creep off the earth—and northward, in Poland, an electrician named Lech, a fellow blue-collar man whose name was synonymous with the blazing flag of Solidarity bannered nightly across the news, put a little light, electric and otherwise, into Europe's dark night; God bless him, those that endured, and those that tried.

In those months, back in our smaller world, was the usual mix of hauteur and pain. On Friday afternoons we gathered outside the office door to watch the new man open his first pay envelope just to see how far his jaw dropped with disbelief that he could work so hard for so little reward. I caught my hand in a roll case, watched it swell to the size of a catcher's mitt, and missed one week of work. Randy caught his hand in a pulley wheel beneath his log deck, broke two fingers and a thumb, and missed six weeks of work. Lightning Joe burned his eyebrows off with a blowtorch, Whiskey-Tim broke a toe and limped for a month, and nearly everyone caught a speck of sawdust beneath his eyelid and swore every time he blinked that a dagger had been thrust into his retina.

In those months we lifted that wounded eye to the commonplace. Carla, the manager's wife, who collected the time cards and kept the books, collared our mirth with her level gaze and gruff dignity at least once a week. Gus, Del, and Henry—the Good Ole Boys—made the journey between the sawmill and the break room eight times a day, always in single file and always slow, as if they were billy goats negotiating a particularly steep mountain pass.

In those months, while we dreamed our plundered dreams, sawdust found every crevice and lined every collar like fur. It clumped in heaps and clung in every weary man's mustache, which is how sawdust smiles.

BELATED AUTHOR'S NOTE

BY NOW, about halfway through these pages, you've likely noticed that these sketches contain no serious swearing or cursing. While many blue-flamed screeds of contempt were produced at the sawmill (for almost anything and at the merest incitement), when it came time to scratch the first bad word onto the bark you're now holding it seemed frivolous to double the length of the manuscript by duplicating that which anyone who hasn't been living under a pallet for twenty years has heard plenty of times already. Along this same plane of logic, I was determined not to teach anything of the numerical aspect of swearing and cursing within the logging industry here.

But for those who insist on knowing how much swearing went on inside a sawmill the matter is simple: get to know a current or former sawmill worker, then count up the number of times he swears or curses in a casual conversation and multiply it by thirty. That will give you a fair idea of how much grass there was to mosey across before you hit mud in a sawmill conversation. My experience was that you hit mud pretty quickly.

During my time in the sawmill, I believed there was a little editor who lived on the back of every mill worker's tongue. This gnomelike personage wore a flannel shirt, stocking cap, and calked boots, looked like the Paul Bunyan from the postage stamp of a decade ago, and was always ready for duty. In fact, when the mill worker was outside the gate in polite society, the little editor was belligerently alert. He sprang quickly to kill all the swear words that passed before him near the back molars, hacking them to pieces with his little ax so he could replace them with more moderate words such as *darn*, *dang-it*, *frick*, and *frig*. The mill worker, whether or not he admitted it, was grateful for this noble service.

But once the mill worker was inside the gate the little editor reversed gears, brutally murdered the darns and dang-its, fricks and frigs, and replaced them with the f-word. He did this with relish. He hacked away as if there were no tomorrow. It was almost as if he were making up for all the tension the moderation outside the fence had caused. In case you haven't noticed, moderation causes tension in those not naturally inclined to it as surely as hot air causes expansion in balloons. In my own case, inside the gate the little editor averaged about one murder per spoken paragraph (not bad, think I). But I worked alongside other men whose every muttered sentence was a triple homicide. Again, just because I have not reproduced evidence of each of these murders in no way implies they didn't occur.

This note is belated so as not to discourage readers who like swearing and cursing.

COME AND GET IT

IN 1880 the stewards of nourishment for lumbermen were the stout, aproned men and women of the cook shanty. In 1980 the grub keepers were the clerks of the local party store and bakery. Neither group, I can say with universal certainty, was interested in your cholesterol level.

I have mentioned the stacker's breakfast, but there was also the stacker's lunch, the stacker's snack, and the stacker's tide over. The breakfast, to review, was a Coca-Cola and a cookie. The stacker's lunch was similar to the breakfast in glucose but heavier in grease, the cookie replaced by two cream-filled cupcakes topped off with three or four strips of beef jerky, a salami stick, and a bag of potato chips. It was enough bad food, in other words, to make even a hound dog queasy.

The stacker's snack, lighter fare, was a Snickers bar at the ten o'clock break and another Coca-Cola at the three o'clock break. The stacker's tide over, for the long journey home after work, was a repeat of the stacker's lunch except the chips were often replaced with cheese curls and on crazy days I sipped a Vernor's instead of a Coke. All told we're talking about a daily intake of four thousand calories but nicely balanced by all those foot-pounds I expended to stack the wood.

I sometimes ask myself if this diet was any worse than the
menu served up by the staff of the cook shanty those many
decades ago. Pancakes, donuts, cookies, pies, heavy syrup,
bacon, and salt pork seem to point to a staffwide indifference toward the health of their clients. Of course I knew
none of these cooks personally, and, to be fair, in the old
photographs they seem more grim than indifferent. But I
knew many convenience store clerks who were both grim
and indifferent and oftentimes worse.

I remember especially the clerk behind the counter of the
Trading Post Party Store, a slender girl of high school age
whose icy touch must have sent more than an occasional
frost across the cash register. One night, after I'd paid for my
Coca-Cola and snack cakes, this girl, obviously repulsed by
my rags and the odor of moldy sawdust I emitted, tossed—
threw might be a better word—my change at me. I tried to
catch the silver as you might field a short hop in baseball,
wincing and pinching my knees together, surprised and put
atremble by the sudden flight of coins. The dime and nickel
glanced off the butt of my hand onto the floor, and each did
a gyroscopic spin before lying flat as sand dollars. After eight
hours of employing the technique to stack oak railroad ties,
it was no easy feat to bend for the money; the nickel I
plucked readily enough, but the dime resisted my touch and
whatever finesse was left in wood-pulverized fingers. I had to
dive a third time to retrieve it, and for the first time in my
life I understood the phrase "seeing red." The blood pulsed
through my sinus, and my forehead turned hot enough to

melt copper. When I stood up I was dizzy, defeated, and furious all at once. The girl, right on cue, sneered at me. The same girl had just waited pleasantly on a crew of oil-field workers, a gang from the drop forge, and the various and sundry degrees of local carpenters.

"That mill," I heard her hiss to her mother, bringing words and venom together as only a fifteen-year-old girl can. Her mother, the kindly lady who usually waited on us, reprimanded her with a glare and a gentle push aside, though the girl continued to glower.

I thought about this girl and the coins as I stacked the wood the next week. I thought it cosmically unfair that someone so determined to be decent (I'm humbly thinking of myself) should be kicked when he was down—for to be at the sawmill was to be decidedly down—by someone who had never tasted even one bitter clove of sawdust.

"'That mill' is right," I complained to Randy, whose advice was to forget it. But I fussed about it for days, the scourge of self-pity nipping at my fraying edges. Finally, Whiskey-Tim put the entire matter in perspective by saying the whole town thought as much of mill workers and there wasn't a darn thing to be done about it except pack up and exit laughing.

It was much better, delightful in fact, down the road at the D&J Bakery. There, for less than two dollars, you could get a hot pepperoni roll and a cold Pepsi-Cola served up by one of several attractive young women who worked the counter and whose welcoming smiles were set off by wisps of flour on their cheekbones and chins.

The bakery's atmosphere was always friendly and somehow wholesome, made so by the counter staff. I think of them now as angels of the mundane, likely as fed up with their work as I was with mine but with the grace to fold it quietly within their wings. Their easy touch went beyond kneading dough, folding wax paper, and making change. At lunchtime one day, as I stood with my pepperoni roll and soda pop in hand waiting for the Rat and Lanny Boy to catch up, I stared through the frosted window onto the main road through town and for a moment was lost in the reverie of humming motors, idling pedestrians, and falling snow-flakes the size of elm leaves. There was lighthearted conver-sation behind me, and I thought I heard the words "Every-thing will be all right" addressed to me by one of the angels, although to this day I'm unsure if I actually heard or just imagined them. Anyway, there was gentle laughter and a sud-den, hovering presence nearby, and I turned, half expecting to see Jimmy Stewart standing beside me claiming it really was a wonderful life. But it was only the Rat nudging my shoulder, telling me it was time to get back to the sawmill.

SHARPENING

AVE THE SAW FILER STANDS in my memory with his hands dipped in his jeans pockets, a quip about to escape his lip. Dave was quiet, ironic, good natured, reflective, and high strung all at once. Perched on the tall stool beside his workbench, he seemed a vat set down by a higher academy to be tapped for its flow of worldly knowledge.

Dave, who was about forty, seemed to know things your run-of-the-mill sawmill worker didn't. Things to do with taste, tact, who was on the silly path, and who was up on the runners on an even keel. His smile through gritted teeth, the barely perceptible shake or nod of his head, could sway your opinion into a one-eighty spin on nearly any topic. I suppose when you spent your days as Dave did, hammering big blades into balance and filing smaller blades to sharpness, you learned a little bit about what cut it and what did not.

Dave's favorite educational device was the zing. It's difficult to overestimate how big the zing is among young blue-collar workers. A good zing is a payback bullet for someone's foolhardiness without committing the actual murder. A good zing is your defense in a cold, primitive world; if you managed to shoot off one good zing in your sawmill career, you would be as revered as a gunslinger in his prime. A good zing would be talked about for weeks; a great zing would be coronated into legend. At the sawmill Dave the saw filer was the king of zing.

He could zing you with a word, a glance, or—and this was particularly deadly—the way he seemed not to hear your answer to the question he'd just posed to you. He could zing you by calling you a tadpole asshole if you were under twenty-five or a prune-suckin' son of a bitch if you were over forty-five, age demographics with bite. To be around Dave was to know that among us were those who were a nickel short of a quarter, a tooth short of a set, and most people didn't have the sense to point a compass north.

A hundred years ago there is almost no doubt Dave would have been a schoolmaster, dispensing his wisdom in epigrams and aphorisms mixed with enough buckshot humor to keep the kids coming back. He was Horace Mann with a sly grin and a wink. I can picture sharp Dave with his feet up on his desk, his hands clasped behind his head, telling the class that while fools were sometimes a minor spice in life generally it was best to cross over to the opposite sidewalk to avoid them. It was simple, practical advice with an edge.

It's likely Whiskey-Tim and I were under Dave's influence the day the second-grade class marched over from the schoolhouse for a tour of the sawmill. They arrived in brightly colored snowsuits, a waddling troupe of upturned faces following a serious young woman in a long green coat. They were hurried past the green chains and the stacking area and assembled at the north end of the mill, where they were shown the nailing machine, the notcher, and the forklift. All of these things made noise and had moving parts, the things that enthrall children most, and perhaps set their little minds to thinking one day the mill might not be a bad option. To this possibility Tim and I responded from the south end with one word we yelled over and over in the name of education: "Run!"

Dave would have been proud of us.

Sometimes Randy and I spent the morning break with Dave. Randy was certainly up on the runners and holding steady in Dave's esteem, while my view of his view of me was that I had a plug or two of sawdust yet to be brushed from behind my ears. Still, I was nicked by his razor wit only once.

That was the morning Randy decided his saw blade needed changing and reminded me I'd agreed to wheel the thing into the saw-filing room. I don't recall the consenting part, but the actual rolling of a circular steel blade as tall as your chin across twenty yards of concrete and another thirty of bumpy, bark-strewn ground is unforgettable. I remember thinking it was a little like dancing with a large plastic bag of broken glass or daring a big guy with a big knife to cut your throat in that there was no room for a misstep. I remember imagining the pain, the purple, the pus, and the lack of pity I would get for my effort if I happened to roll the thing over my toe. Most of all, I remember the conversation with Dave when I finally eased the blade into the filing room.

"You made it in, eh?" Dave said. In a canvas vest, a flannel shirt, and a cap pushed back on his forehead, Dave was always dressed like a bass fisherman.

"I made it in," I said.

"Did you get bit?"

"Nope."

"That's good," Dave said. "It's always nice to get a dangerous job out of the way."

"It is," I agreed.

"Have you stopped shaking yet?"

"I'm not bad."

"That's good," Dave said. He seemed to draw a breath and hiccup silently at the same time. Then he said, "You're not daunted by a damn thing, are you?"

Thrilled that I'd fooled Dave with my hollow confidence, I thought it over a half second too long and said, "Nope."

"That's good," Dave said, and pointed to a freshly hammered blade on the table. "Now you get to wheel that sweetheart back."

THE FOREMAN

BIG TOM THE FOREMAN STARES calmly out of the past, a friendly, hulking figure of about thirty-five. Tom was built like a railroad tie set on top of an icebox, in other words, like a small warehouse, although neither analogy does justice to the girth of his shoulders. I associate Tom with the day at the sawmill I wanted to do good. Good in the biblical sense, good in the philosophical sense, good in any sense you could think of. At this job that paid pullets, stretched my limbs, and put slivers behind my fingernails, I wanted simply, directly, and finally to do good. It was urgent. The truth is I didn't understand it at all.

That morning, after I reminded him that we needed twenty-one stacks to make the load—twenty-one stacks of popple cants would fill the flatbed of a semitrailer, five double stacks down each side and one directly behind the cab—Big Tom the foreman shrugged those bulky shoulders and said, "Don't worry."

When I leaped onto the runner of the forklift a minute later, unconvinced that Tom had gotten the message, and told him, *lied* to him, that I needed to be out the gate for an appointment at 5:00 p.m.—five having become my goal, my reckoning of what would constitute good—Big Tom said it again: "Don't worry."

But I worried; I couldn't help it. I worried because Big Tom was in charge of the daily operation of the mill and because his humped posture wasn't exactly caused by the weight of his intellect (I was no brighter than Tom, of course, but I didn't know that then). To make matters worse, he was a relative of the manager—a galloping case of nepotism—with the highly resented privilege of being generally unaccountable for his actions.

Not that Tom wasn't a nice guy—a veteran of combat in Vietnam, he seemed remarkably unassuming—but under his watch the operation had become sloppy. Workers showed up late (or not at all), machinery broke down, and oak was dropped onto the decks when the load called for popple. The mill yard had become a clutter of sawdust piles, pallet rows, and heaps of scrap wood, a yard that with the spring thaw had lost whatever quaint Rockwellian qualities it had and had taken on the settle and sprawl of neglect. I worried because, although Big Tom had the wheel of the forklift in his hand and as foreman had the final say in a sawmill equipped with two large head saws that could pare one-ton logs to the size of Lincoln Logs in minutes, we hadn't gotten a load out by five o'clock in two weeks, a fortnight of futility.

And sure enough, precedent jumped up and shouted. By first break that morning, we had built exactly one and a half stacks, and Big Tom, from the forklift, said, "Don't worry." At noon we had a measly five stacks, and again Big Tom said it was nothing to worry about.

In the truck at lunchtime—well out of earshot—I berated Big Tom. Randy quietly agreed that Big Tom was inept, unqualified, and elevated by blood in a clan where blood meant nothing, but he also took a moment to eye me and ask why having the load out by five o'clock mattered so much. I gave a shrug, mumbled something about being fed up, and left it at that. I really didn't have an answer. All I knew was that the work day was moving much too slowly, and in a place where so much was round—fan belts, saw blades, forklift tires—and by implication fast, slowness was pure torture. The outline of good was there, but we might as well have been trying to touch Mars with a toothpick.

As I sat in the truck, not quite believing the primary goal in my life was to get a load of popple cants out by five o'clock, I felt an unexpected calm. For just a heartbeat, quiet had so engulfed the mill yard that I believe something like acceptance had descended. And then from the edges of the silence came a ringing, and I thought of those five pitiful stacks and all those left to build, and when the crew emerged from the break room and the other vehicles in the parking lot, the ringing became a buzz, the buzz a grind that blew to a roar, and the next thing I knew I was in the mill again and the wood was coming.

It thundered down the roll cases and tumbled onto the green chains as if snapped from a blanket, a veritable river of large, vanilla-colored, slightly gleaming popple cants. Because we had stacked an astronomical amount of lumber, Whiskey-Tim and I watched the wood come toward us as a running stag watches the bank of the stream approach and knows, gauges, the precise moment to leap. And we leaped.

Pull, turn, step, set, slide.

We stacked and stacked. All the while Big Tom the foreman, riding his forklift—an ogre on a burro—hauled the cants to the flatbed. The clock turned, the wood piled up, but I had stopped counting stacks at noon. As we worked, Whiskey-Tim was mired in his love gloom for Cheri, while I thought about everything under the sun: my beloved, baseball, beer, food, beer, baseball, and food. I was thinking about all of these things when the saws and chipper went down in unison. The change in the atmospheric pressure in the mill seemed to lift my chin, and when I looked up and saw the crew headed out of the mill for break time I also saw Big Tom maneuvering the forklift toward the flatbed and the popple stacks there for the counting. So I counted. When I finished, I counted again to double-check my math. The last break was upon us, and we were at seventeen!

A long time has passed since the moment when I knew we would beat the clock and good would happen. Now I think I understand why I needed to get that load out on time and what Big Tom the foreman had to do with that need. Now I see that there was a line in the yard—invisible at the time—and on one side was me, the revulsion I felt toward the mill, and my determination to keep it at a distance. That side of the line represented the world the way I wanted it to be. On the other side of the line was Big Tom the foreman. Big Tom represented the world the way it is, the world that bulked your shoulders, lined your face, and plastered you with dross and a hangdog expression, the world that was utterly sloppy and had never once stopped at five o'clock. That was Big Tom's world, and I wanted no part in it.

Of course I was wrong. It was all one world, and now, when I remember Tom standing in that world saying "Don't worry," I also hear the implication of what I was deaf to then: "it's not that bad." And I know during that time when I wanted so badly to get away, the thing that was so urgent, that was my desire, was simple enough: I wanted to be innocent just one more day. Big Tom, nice man that he was, was telling me in his own way not to be so naive. He knew our world better than I did, and I had no business judging whether or not he was competent in it.

After the break we cut two more stacks, and Tom found two more under a tarp in the yard. The thing was done by four-thirty, although in some ways that long ago day ends only as I write this. To the foreman, wherever you are, I would like to say I'm sorry and, without further ado, thank you.

THE TREE LOVER

PATRICK LOVED trees. He was a tall, pumpkin-haired kid of eighteen, who, on his first morning at the mill, introduced himself around like the ill-at-ease new kid at school who wants the awkwardness of a first week to be compressed into a few minutes and then be over, a classic case of the primordial ache.

That morning Patrick held a bit of nervous court at the scrap wood bin, a rusted tub of corrugated metal where anything from Coca-Cola cans to shredded bark was tossed. The scrap wood bin was a gathering place much on the order of an office water cooler. You could lean against one side of the bin while Whiskey-Tim, Lanny Boy, or Skinny Eddie did likewise against the other, and the enforced distance was perfect for a sawmill conversation. Whenever there was a lull in the talk, you only had to gaze down into the bin and another topic would replenish your mind like a cool drink from a stone well.

Patrick loomed over the bin as if at a lectern and talked and gestured like a young man settling in. Among other things, he told us that he loved trees and was taking classes at a local community college to become a forester. I wished

Patrick hardy days at the mill but couldn't help thinking he was in the wrong place for his dream and wondered if, instead of viewing the loads of timber being trucked in through the gate as potential pallets, he saw them as slaughtered prodigy. Sooner or later wouldn't it occur to him that the beautiful wood he was using to build a stack had left behind a withering remnant, that somewhere there was a stump and its roots in a woodland version of rigor mortis? Whatever he might have been thinking, it was certainly with a concerned eye that he scanned the mill yard.

I remember that his orange hair wisped along the collar of his army surplus jacket and he wore a marijuana leaf belt buckle and drove a Volkswagen, a gentle free spirit behind barbed wire. It couldn't last. He worked at the mill for two weeks, quit, and we forgot about him. Two months later in the backseat of the Blazer on the drive to work, I suddenly sat bolt upright, having made the connection that a young man I'd read about in the paper the week before who had been killed when his small car was crushed by a truck was the same Patrick, lover of trees.

STOICS

GUS, DEL, AND HENRY STAND along the mill wall of my memory ready to form a column at a moment's notice. The Good Ole Boys were famous for walking in single file between the mill and the break room several times a day, a perfect example of workingmen marching to the drumbeat of habit. In winter they dodged the small patches of dark ice and threaded their way across the mill yard tundra with their heads bent against the cold; in spring they moved in grumpy silence around the enormous puddle the rains and melted snow had left in the yard, a body of water known as Fluffy's Lake in sarcastic homage to its owner; in summer their steps brought up small explosions of dust, which mushroomed and fell feebly away at their heels; and in autumn the yard was firm and passable with hardly a scuff to their boots. But regardless of whether the yard relented or not, the Good Ole Boys crossed it in single file, a centipede of older men heading in either direction to its hole in the wall. They moved in single file, I think, for the same reason that geese fly in a *V*, whatever that reason is. Henry almost always led the way, followed by Del and then Gus.

It was Randy who knighted them the Good Ole Boys, although only Henry was close to retirement age. He was a brittle fellow with a rickety walk who might have been anywhere between fifty-eight and ninety-eight years old. There seemed to be stone weights tugging down the corners of his mouth, stretching the rest of his face into a sheen of contempt for anything that wasn't flag, company, or Richard Nixon.

Nobody at the mill had more seniority than Henry, although no one seemed to know quite how much that was. Henry had been with the operation when it was located up in Kalkaska, or had been with some operation or other in Kalkaska, and was lured down to the mill in Lake City because of his supposed prowess with the cutoff saw. According to Randy, Henry sat in the break room one morning and reminded everyone within earshot that the owner of the mill had asked him specifically to come down and run this saw. Apparently Henry uttered this line with the solemnity you would utter "General MacArthur asked me to lead the charge up Pork Chop Hill." For Henry to act as if he were a gem of stolen talent when by all accounts a monkey could run the cutoff saw caused Randy no small disgust. I agreed that for old Henry to think himself a sawyer just because his saw had a blade and cut wood was a bit far-fetched; on the other hand I thought a few minutes of Henry letting the sun warm his self-image was harmless.

Another bothersome thing about Henry was that he let his wife ask for his pay raises. Every few months Mrs. Henry (as she was known, though not to her or Henry's face) would pull through the gate in the family Buick and, with bravado that appalled nearly everyone, park smack dab next to the company pickup. While Henry hid in the mill, Mrs. Henry would climb from the Buick—a flyer from the local super-market in hand—and march into the manager's office. Her negotiation technique was simple but guilt inducing: point out the price of bread and milk and ask the manager how he would like to pay such outrageous prices on Henry's wage.

The manager, so the story goes, would counter with a la-ment about how bad business was, how the mill was barely keeping its windows above the economic pond scum, but after a little wearing down from Mrs. Henry he would say to heck with it. Mrs. H. would emerge from the office with a nickel or dime raise for her man, her face agleam with triumph.

Math was never my lollipop, but I did the math on this one. A nickel got the Henry family a hundred bucks a year before taxes. Meanwhile, Henry himself, widely known as a company man and the polar opposite of a rabble-rouser, would lose four years off the end of his life out of sheer angst over his wife's visits. On these days Henry actually seemed to shrink. He'd huddle in the mill, stamp his feet to keep his blood circulating, and sneak wary glances through the big door toward the office. When the Buick finally pulled out, he'd stop wringing his hands and ease back up to his normal height. I saw this with my own eyes and couldn't believe that what the poor man went through was worth a thousand dollars much less a hundred. But he was a happy gander afterward and soared back to his work as if to prove he was worth every nickel his wife had bargained for.

Del was a quiet man of forty-two who ate a cheese sandwich every day for lunch. Del's job was to stack the boards and runners that quivered out the back end of the gang saw, wood that was then used to build pallets. Of course over on the green chains we didn't consider this real stacking. In our unbiased opinion, boards and runners were bush league toting compared to lifting cants and railroad ties. If the stacking didn't shrivel your spleen and points south, it wasn't considered worthy of the name. Sure, some foot-pounds were being accumulated, but it was entry-level stacking at best. Gang saw stacking involved an awful lot of bending, however, and Del had trouble with his back (maybe all the cheese was to replenish his calcium level). He walked with his legs far apart, feet slightly ducked, and very slowly, as if the ice were always about to give way beneath him.

Del was Whiskey-Tim's brother-in-law and the one who got Tim the job at the sawmill. They didn't get on well, and, while I never knew the specifics of their rift, I suspect it had something to do with Del having gotten Whiskey-Tim the job. Occasionally one would walk up to tell me how lazy the other one was. Whiskey-Tim wasn't a lick lazy, of course, although toward the end of his time at the mill he was often distracted. Del wasn't lazy, either, and now that I'm somewhere near his age then I would certainly buy the argument that he was pacing himself. In fact, in Del's exhausted stride and bend there was a kind of elegance, as if he were quietly spreading tablecloths or setting out towels in a four-star hotel. In a company town of a hundred years ago, I can imagine him as the sweep-up man in the boardinghouse, the man who kept the place clean and the mice away, the weary but competent man with the broom, all of which would have required pacing, bending, and cheese.

Gus was forty-six years old, although when I first knew him he looked sixty if he looked a day, which is what life at the mill could do to you even when you were careful. Gus was the friendliest of the Good Ole Boys, the one you could count on to say hello and stroll over for a chat. One day we stood in the big entrance and watched as Whiskey-Tim tried to kick a big chunk of slabwood through the chipper. The chipper was making a tinny, ringing noise, which meant the blades had dulled, and Tim was kicking hard and precariously close to the opening, trying to get the blades to grab the wood and suck it through. After a minute, Gus said, "Won't be long 'fore his nickname is Stumpy." You had to be there, maybe, but it was darned funny.

For a few weeks one summer, Gus's oldest son worked in the mill. A recent high school graduate, he was biding time building pallets before he took the army's entrance exam. He was a nice kid (and twice the size of Gus) with his father's friendly bearing and gift for easy conversation. Unfortunately, he flunked the exam, which meant a longer stint at the mill than he'd planned. Neither Gus nor his son ever confessed as much, but the failure must have been a blow to them. You could see it in their faces, the glum, exasperated look of good people who would get over it but were hurting. I remember one afternoon when, as the Good Ole Boys were headed out of the mill for break time, Gus suddenly stepped out of line, quickened his pace, and briskly passed Del and Henry on their way to the break room. Randy and I watched from the Blazer in disbelief. In Gus's stride was the determination of Seattle Slew headed down the backstretch. It was as if he were saying that he was capable of taking the point, of leading the way, of kicking up dust until he got the results he wanted. Somewhere in that stretch, I suspect the seed of a pep talk or an ultimatum for his son was planted, for the next day Gus fell back in line and looked more content than I'd seen him in days.

It's unlikely that Gus, Del, or Henry would have put it quite this way, but I'm sure they felt more virtuous in the classical sense than the younger crew did. And, although I would not have been able to define the terms then, I would have agreed with them. Inside the fence they seemed to possess a degree of prudence, fortitude, and temperance that we on the green chains, the surly lumber stackers, did not. While it might be that at their ages the hard physical labor had rendered them too weary to misbehave, their good behavior still counts as virtuous. In my estimation all these years later, experience had made them prudent, necessity had given them fortitude, and age had made them temperate. They were just fellows, too, in the Platonic sense, meaning they seemed to move with a balance of reason, spirit, and appetite. We younger workers struggled with the balance. The appetite for license was like a roaring lion that only reason and spirit, the chair and whip as it were, could tame. But appetite often won. Appetite is what caused Lanny Boy to pull the cotter pin out of a link in the green chains, which knotted the chains around the sprocket and shut down the entire operation on the south end for three hours. Appetite is what caused Whiskey-Tim to allow three of the most gorgeous cherry-wood boards we had ever seen to be eaten by the chipper and spit into the chip van in a million pieces. Appetite is what caused me to scratch "Fluffy Sucks" on the back of my hard-hat, a disparaging reference to the mill's owner, a dutiful, un-assuming man and competent heir to his father's modest empire.

But the appetite for license never ruled the day at the mill because (although we wouldn't have admitted it) we did now and then cast a glance at Gus, Del, and Henry, and knew, I think, deep down in the sawdust pit of our hearts, that the Good Ole Boys knew a better way.

THE TATTOO MAN

UNTIL A MONTH before it occurred, the Tattoo Man's departure from the sawmill would have caused me to pump a fist into the air in relief and triumph. Although he'd passed me free drinks at the Christmas party many moons before, he'd proven gruff, lazy, and intimidating, not the ideal workmate. None of this, however, stopped him from believing he was the most lovable pup on earth.

The Tattoo Man was equal parts hippie burnout and playground bully. He carried a hammer to look busy, chased off meeklings like Lanny Boy to do the heavy work he didn't want to do himself, and leaned against the scrap wood bin to smoke marijuana in full view of everyone, convinced, I suppose, that it fostered his image as a radical. He spoke in a low, hoarse voice, mumbling "cools," "far outs," and the f-word from a throat raw with vice, the rasp of a man in his eighties rather than his twenties. Whiskey-Tim told us that parties at the Tattoo Man's house were orgies of acid, alcohol, and adultery that ended far into the night, usually with the Tattoo Man face down on the floor in his own vomit. Every morning on our way to the mill, I prayed that the Tattoo Man would be arrested and sent to prison, prayed fervently that his sentence would last as long as it took me to leave the mill myself. It made me cringe to think of him strutting through the gate again as if the mill were his conquered territory.

But, as with my first impression of most of my work-mates at the sawmill, I was wrong about the Tattoo Man. And when he had finally departed for good, his druggy fog in tow, I thought the real man had only recently come forth.

The change showed on a warm, windy day in April as we stacked the wood outdoors. After the morning break, the Tattoo Man appeared in the big entrance, surveying the scene with his groggy stare. For a moment he seemed hesitant, but then, removing his jacket, he started down the drive toward me. Suddenly my stomach felt tighter than it did the morning I'd squelched goofy Schultzie. For a long time I felt the Tattoo Man had been sizing me up, and now, at last, he had me figured for someone who could be cowed. The truth is, with his stout chest, shag haircut, goatee, and mustache, as well as his general Detroit Rock City look, I was daunted by the Tattoo Man. But I was ready. I thought I'd do all right if I had to. I just hoped not to have to.

Then something unexpected happened. In retrospect, maybe I should have expected it, because it now seems in cosmic ordinance with the warm wind and gusts of golden sawdust sprinkling down from the roof. The Tattoo Man said my name. Not my last name, not some vulgar nickname, but the name my mother and father and grandmothers and siblings called me. My name rose into the spring air and floated like a pious butterfly.

At that moment I knew the Tattoo Man had some decency after all. Simple, honest decency, even when I realized it was less cosmic than commerce. The Tattoo Man was preparing to sell. In the span of a minute, he went from lazy mill hand to aggressive salesman. His products, produced by his own hand, were the tattoos on his blighted forearms: a pirate's sword that looked like a butter knife and a cobra with coils so thick it looked more like a stack of old tires than a snake. The Tattoo Man wondered if I wanted one. That was why he'd said my name so gently, why he was a mountain lion when he jumped off the crag but Mary Poppins when he landed. I was a prospective customer. No, I wasn't even a customer (the tattoo would be free after all); I was a guinea pig, a chunk of canvas, or something like it, for the druggy fog turned out to be an artistic dream and the Tattoo Man needed the practice.

All I had to do was sit still, the deal you gave a weed before you took the whacker to it. To stall I said I'd need time to think it over, but the Tattoo Man's eyes were gleaming. It was his dream to open his own parlor. When he told me this, the words *opium den* jumped to mind, but I pushed them aside. The Tattoo Man was saving money for rent on a little shop and the inventory to put in it—gun, ink, needles, and so on—but needed the practice to become licensed. I looked down at his tattoos again—hardly better than finger drawings on the dusty fender of a pickup—and repeated that I'd have to think about it. But when he began to plead, I knew begging and groveling weren't far behind. Finally I told him I'd had hepatitis as a child and that to be poked with even the smallest needle could prove lethal. The latter was my own and not an official medical opinion but no less true. With this the Tattoo Man relented. He drew back and told

me he was sorry to hear it. Tattoos were the thing, he said.
He then rolled down his sleeves as if closing the garage doors
on a couple of Mercedes. He said if I knew anyone who
wanted a tattoo to let him know and remember to tell them
it was free.

A hundred years ago I think the Tattoo Man would have
been a gambling man. He had a lust for success and an even
lustier belief that he possessed the wit to attain it. I can picture him descending the staircase from the upper floor of the
local saloon after a dalliance with one of the working girls,
fingering the stash in his belt, dressed in his best white shirt,
red vest, trim black jacket, and fine string tie, his hat tipped
just so to keep his face hidden in shadow. Instead of his
cheesy little goatee, he would have sported a horseshoe
mustache and wide sideburns tapered to points as sharp as a
peavey. He would have moved with the air of a man who
believed he carried special knowledge of hearts, clubs and
spades, knowledge that if used just right could fill your
pockets with gold in even the remotest sawmill town.

With one boot up on the brass rail of the long oak bar, a
pistol glint in his eye, he would have slugged down a shot of
rye and wandered over for a chat with the piano player before heading off to the tables. There, in 1880, his hand full of
cardboard diamonds, the Tattoo Man would have created
the aura of a winner and behaved much better than he did at
his real life poker games of 1980. With his realm the Golden
Dust Saloon and not some squalid rental, there would have
been an expectation of better behavior: no more sex in door-
ways and dancing on the furniture, no more reefer and acid,
no more howling at the moon. The Golden Dust might

have smelled of a mix of beer and French perfume (imported directly from Canada) but not of vomit and license. It would have been a joint a lumberjack could go to for a respectable good time, and the Tattoo Man would have thought of himself as its gambling prince. I can imagine him smiling as Whiskey-Tim stepped up to the bar, saying he hadn't seen such a nice watering hole since his cathouse days in Nevada. I can imagine his relief when the Cat grumbled that it was too nice a place in which to spill blood. I can even imagine his mirth when Lightning Joe used the place to show off his shiny spurs. But most of all I can imagine the Tattoo Man, finding his stash much depleted—he wouldn't have drawn aces any better than tattoos—ponying up his pride to buy a round for the house. It's a romantic notion of the Tattoo Man, I know, but it doesn't seem far-fetched, and it's by far more favorable to think of him passing out drinks, as he once did for me, rather than simply passing out.

Not long after his offer to decorate me, the Tattoo Man fluttered away to work in a union shop. I was happy for him. That was a dream of his, too.

THE RAT

BECAUSE OF THE WAY HE RAN with his wrists held limply to his chest and his elbows tucked to his sides, the chief nailer was nicknamed the Rat. The round brown eyes, the wispy mustache, and the overlapping front teeth only added to the effect.

The Rat was the most sardonic man at the sawmill. A newcomer assigned to the nailing machine was subjected to a barrage of questions from him, beginning with "Did your parents have any children that lived?" and running on to an approximate end with "Why does your grandma walk like that?" The questions in between were nastier.

A half hour on the nailing machine made you more defensive than a grub on a roller rink, but that was by the Rat's design. He was basically a democrat and knew a dose of defensiveness attuned you to the gristle and groan of the workaday world, the world we all lived in whether we wanted to admit it or not. The Rat felt it was his duty to remind you of this in case you were one of the drones who had conveniently forgotten it. If his manner and method didn't exactly come off as concern for your feelings, well, that was life at the sawmill.

Despite the pummeling your ego took, it was hard not to like the Rat. You liked him for the way he used a kind of wile to keep the old wreck of a nailing machine—it resembled a cross between a colonial printing press and the bed of a Ford pickup—up and running. He gave the thing a frequent adjusting, greasing, and cajoling to produce a daily load of pallets, which was the point of the mill's existence (not its employees' misery) to begin with. With his mechanical skill and face-to-the-wind enthusiasm, it's hard to imagine the Rat being anything but an engineer on one of the numerous narrow-gauge railroad systems that scratched the forest back in the lumbering era. The whole idea of levers to be pulled, measurements to be taken, schedules to keep, gauges and gadgets to tinker with, noise to be made, and the general grit, grime, and laughter would have been an overwhelming attraction to him.

You liked him because he was the perfect guy through whom to gather a sense of the preposterousness, the riotousness, of the real world at work and a sense of the industriousness and fortitude necessary to deal with it. He was the monarch of the north end of the mill, and like a true monarch there was an element of fatalism in his makeup. The Rat's perspective was that if kings could be dethroned, disgraced, and beheaded then what could you expect as a peasant? You couldn't expect much, really, so the best course was simply to carry on, boisterously if possible. It was a lesson with an inherent hardness, but the delivery from the Rat's twitching mustache was oddly endearing.

You liked him because on lunch breaks he'd drive the nailing crew to his house to play pinball in his basement, offering up Coca-Colas to boot, and because he told the best sick joke you had ever heard in your life, which will not be repeated here. But the main reason you liked the Rat was because beneath the crust of sarcasm, hard and shiny as it was, you sensed he was a decent guy. Sure, the jokes were vulgar and the chiding rash, but you felt it was a wing, a prickly one, but a wing nonetheless, that you were being brought under. And it wasn't as if he'd lowered himself to take you in; that wasn't it at all. He'd simply never considered himself above you in the first place. I sensed this the few times I worked on the nailing machine, even as my mother was accused of mating with an orangutan.

And it—the Rat's humility—turned out to be genuine. During my last autumn at the mill, his first child, a daughter, was born with a faulty heart and died within a few hours. The next morning the Rat showed up at the mill to see if the load was getting out. Whiskey-Tim and I happened to be headed for the break room when the Rat walked through the gate. He wore clean blue jeans, a dress shirt, and a jean jacket, in mill parlance dressed up and respectable. And in that open yard, under the big northern sky, you could see the sarcasm was gone from his face, replaced with something like sheepishness. Most clearly what you saw was that the Rat wasn't a rat but a guy named Gerry.

We tapped our toes in the dust and told him we were sorry about the baby, and he thanked us. He told us his wife was blaming herself, and we almost said that was crazy but caught ourselves and said that wasn't right instead. Gerry said that's what he'd told her. We said there would be another chance, and he agreed there would be. He had to be thinking, this decent, hardworking man who, day after day, week after week, rigged and tickled, hammered and twisted an old bolt box until it worked, that they could put a man on the moon, measure the depths of the oceans, and build buildings into the sky, but they couldn't keep one little two-ounce heart beating. But he didn't say it. We told him to take care, and he said he would. There was an awkward pause before Gerry roused himself and said, "I'd better get." We told him to take care again and watched him go. His grief must have weighed like an anvil, but he didn't say that either. He was from the old school, or rather, the old mill, the one of long-suffering silence. For a moment an image flashes in my mind of all those jacks, bullwhackers, and lumber stackers in photographs, real or imagined, standing and cheering for Gerry.

The little girl's name was Dorothy.

THE TRANSIENT

O NE MORNING the Transient appeared at the end of
the green chains, employing the technique on oak
cants as if he'd been doing it his whole life. No one seemed
to know his name or where he was from, although Whiskey-
Tim heard that he'd worked in sawmills all over the Great
Lakes. The Transient was enigmatic, a wanderer. I could
never think of him as anything less than the ghost of the
future.

He looked to be about forty-five years old, of medium
build, his face chiseled like the bark of an old stump. He wore
thick, black-frame glasses and the usual ragged clothing:
fingerless gloves, dress shoes of the accountant-on-skid-row
variety, and a plaid flannel jacket. As lumber stackers go, he
was nondescript.

What wasn't nondescript was that he rode to work on a
florescent lemon-colored bicycle. So bright was the paint job
on this bike that it practically required sunglasses to look at
it. No one had ever ridden a bike to the mill before, let alone
one that cut the morning dim so loudly. The Transient
leaned it against the fence without bothering to chain or
lock it, an object that screamed, "Steal me," if ever one did,

though sad would have been the criminal element that undertook the dare.

If his bike seemed out of place, the Transient himself fit like a description of the spring's restlessness: nameless, darting, unmoored. Most days he worked with the nailing crew, but now and then he'd turn up at the chain to toss a cant or two onto a stack. There was something in the way he put too much weight on his heels, in the slouch of his shoulders, and in the way he bound himself so intently to the task at hand— almost as if to deny the larger world—that reminded me of myself. He certainly had the contradictory aura of the stacker's desire: to work hard and be somewhere else. In that respect he was just like the rest of the crew.

We spoke only once. One morning, with a steady flow of pine boards about to command the chain, he asked me if we separated the white pine from the red. I wasn't sure I knew the difference between white and red pine, but I was sure it didn't matter, so I told him to stack 'em all together. The Transient nodded with a dip of his jaw, turned, and walked away. I learned later that red pine retained more water than white and was therefore risky as furniture stock, something the Transient likely knew but decided not to impart to me. Maybe all those foot-pounds had smothered my judgment, maybe I was mill-weary, maybe the Transient now had me figured for someone who didn't know a tree limb from a trombone, but I thought I'd given an intelligent answer.

One Friday night, as we drove into town to cash our pay-checks, we noticed the fluorescent bike leaned against the wall of the W. H. Hotel, a crumbling, century-old structure that was a haven for the dispossessed. The next week we saw the bike outside the Town Pump Bar. Both times the bike was like a bolt of electricity in the dusk trying to switch on a light in my head. I began to wonder how a life could come to living in a rundown hotel, socializing at the local bar, riding a secondhand bicycle to work in a sawmill, and nothing else. Before coming to the mill, I would have considered such a life romantic. I thought you could choose your own worldly circumstances, inserting and extracting yourself from them at will. Now, observing the Transient, I thought it less romantic than desolate, that maybe you didn't get to choose after all, that you could become stuck in your circumstances and then be swallowed by them. It scared me a little. Maybe more than a little.

After only a couple of weeks, the Transient left the mill. I imagined the hiss of bus brakes, a door opening and closing, a departure as obscure as his life. Driving through town one night we noticed the bike leaned against the hotel wall. A chain was wound through the spokes, and across the handlebars someone had balanced a "For Sale" sign.

FIRST MILL

VIRGIL THE JAILBIRD, the Blue Old Man, and Pouty Marv linger in my memory with the yellow-eyed owner of my first mill, ghostly wisps from the summer after high school. Their gaze lingers heavily too, wounded, maybe, that I'd almost forgotten them.

Virgil was a straw-haired ruffian with a sliver neck and wafer thin shoulders who was spending the off hours of his summer in the county jail for stealing television sets and kitchen appliances from tourist cabins around Higgins Lake. The first day I ever spent at a sawmill was across a jig table from Virgil nailing pallets together. I was awkward with the nailing gun, but Virgil was forgiving, for I was not only the new man, I was someone new with whom to talk. The company up at the jailhouse (his "legal company"), he complained, was becoming stale.

Virgil never talked about his specific crime, only his serve time. In jail, he said, you dreamed of all the simple things you did before you were locked up, dreams so vivid you believed events and convictions in them to be real. There were mornings, for instance, when he felt hung over, other mornings he felt he'd been carnal with someone the night before, and many, many mornings, while building pallets, when he felt it would have been a perfectly legal act to walk out the gate in search of work he really liked. But Virgil knew better. From 7:00 a.m. to 5:30 p.m., Monday through Friday, he was a ward of the mill owner, who judiciously sent someone by the jig table every half hour to make sure Virgil hadn't acted on his dreams.

What I remember best about Virgil is his supplicant's posture as he waited beside the road in front of the mill for his lunch to be delivered. Every day at noon a squad car would ease down the hill, silent as a slipper on hardwood, and pull to a stop just as the window came down far enough for the deputy to hand out a brown paper bag. Inside was Virgil's feast: a peanut butter sandwich and a wilted orange, delicacies for which the county charged him five dollars a day. Virgil complained bitterly about the price, though not in the presence of the deputies. When the deputy had handed him the bag, Virgil would say, "Thank you, mom," and the deputy would reply with two words, the second of which was "you," roll up the window, and drive away.

One morning at the jig table Virgil suddenly paused, rested his nailing gun on the table, and stared at me. His eyes were wide, and his mouth hung like a change slot. His stillness was so profound you half believed a bolt of revelation had just powdered him. "Freedom," he said, as if tasting the word on his tongue for the first time, "there's nothing like it." Then he went back to building pallets.

Standing next to Virgil in my memory of that first mill is Pouty Marv. He was built of hardly more than the baggy clothes on his back, his long jaw settled into a pout that only somewhat blunted the sad peak of his brow. Pouty Marv was a tad slow but gentle as a cottontail bunny. This naturally made him a target of jokes and high jinks and very often a victim of unbridled contempt.

One afternoon a couple of hands with hambones for brains took Pouty Marv to the back wall of the mill and with air guns nailed him to the planks by the borders of his clothing. As Marv hung a foot off the floor, one of the rogues took a nail and carved a half dozen horseshoe shapes onto each side of his face. Then, as his clothing plucked from the nails one by one and looking as though he had a severe case of ringworm, Marv more or less folded onto the floor. His weltered face was a portrait of strangled rage as he lifted himself up and whimpered through the dark laughter out of the mill.

He was gone all afternoon, the following day, and the day after that. Rumor had it he was never coming back, a rumor so filled with accusing light that the dark hearts squirmed in regret. After a week, the collective guilt having scorched both perpetrators and observers, we piled into a pickup, drove up the main road through town, and found Marv in a donut shop. The Cat, who plied some of his smiling wrath at this mill, too, was the spokesman. The rest of us fanned out behind him, the saddest contingent of diplomats ever assembled. The Cat's terms were that if Marv would stop being a fool and come back to the mill where he belonged we'd forgive him for ignoring us a whole week without notice. It was undeniable that Marv had the better bargaining position.

He looked at home among the tables full of pensioners, re-
tirees, and local good old boys, and all the old men seemed
just as comfortable with him. But when the Cat offered up
his services as a personal protector, Marv's jaw worked hard
to push back a grin. He felt obliged to put on a bit of a front,
and in his drawling voice kept repeating, "Well, I don't
know, I just don't know," but the next day he showed up at
the mill and another whole week passed before anyone
picked on him again.

From the incident with Marv, I learned that I should put a
penny in the peanut machine of compassion now and then,
before things went too far. But from the episode with the
Blue Old Man, I learned it's sometimes the correct thing to
keep the penny in your pocket.

   The Blue Old Man was around sixty and thin as a green
bean. I thought of him as the Blue Old Man not only because
his eyes were the color of a jay's feather and he always wore
blue jeans and blue work shirts with the sleeves rolled to the
elbows, but also because the bend in his shoulders seemed to
be caused by the weight of an unrelenting melancholy.

   One Monday morning the Blue Old Man failed to show
up for work, and on Tuesday, as punishment, the foreman
assigned him the arduous if not downright gruesome task of
stacking pallets. Stacking pallets was decidedly a young man's
game, ideally a young man with twice the girth and strength
of the Blue Old Man. That summer we built many loads for
the regional Pepsi-Cola distributor, in particular heavy, cumbersome pallets of wet oak weighing ninety spleen-writhing

pounds apiece. To move this pallet the stacker had to lift it directly up from the slots in the jig table, set it on end to gain a better grip, and then carry it several yards to the stacking area. The initial lift out of the jig was the stacker's biggest obstacle, for the angle was simply evil in its elimination of leverage and physics as helpmates. Fortunately, being eighteen years old and one who was later told he was strong as a horse, I could stack Pepsi pallets ten hours a day in ninety-degree heat, but the Blue Old Man, whose usual job was stacking boards behind the gang saw, was in up to his hernia. The nailers, an impatient lot, often had to help him pry the pallet from its snug fit in the jig, grumbling the whole time it took for the Blue Old Man to pull the pallet up on end, get his tenuous grip, and then walk with it to the stack. From the moment he lifted the pallet from the jig table, his spine formed a perfect letter *C*, his legs so burdened with the weight that they moved, heartbreakingly, as if from static electricity. This went on for a couple of hours before the foreman stopped being a dupe to his twisted sense of propriety and sent the Blue Old Man back behind the gang saw. For maybe the only time at that mill, I gladly took over the pallet stacking.

At day's end we drove up behind the Blue Old Man as he slogged up the incline of the road toward the main road, where he lived in a run-down hotel.

"Should we give him a lift?" I asked Randy.

"Naw."

"He's had a bad day; why not?"

I had already sucked in the air to call to the Blue Old Man, but Randy said, "Don't do it."

As we drove even with him, the Blue Old Man flashed us a look of blue fire that angled any lower might have melted the engine block of Randy's rusty Impala.

"He don't want your sympathy," Randy said. I didn't have to ask what the Blue Old Man did want because Randy added, "He just wants to be left alone," and that ended the matter. Randy was twenty-one years old but possessed a knack well beyond his years for reading the blue heart of a workingman. As we passed by, the Blue Old Man looked down at the ground and settled into the walk toward his peace.

I worked at my first mill six weeks and then quit to take a month off before I went to college. I slept the month away, or at least that's how I remember it. The weariness rolled over me like amber waves of sawdust, a combination of fatigue pent up from the heat, the heavy work, the late nights, and the relief of finally being released from it all. Randy, however, had no time to sleep away. He quit the same day and two weeks later went to work at what would become our second mill.

GRUNTS

THERE ARE other wood grunts I think of often. There was No-Doubt Brian, who always said "No doubt" to mean "Yes" and possessed long, elegant fingers that might have belonged to a concert pianist or been famous in a cigarette advertisement. (This fixation on fingers must stem from the always real chance of losing one and from the safety posters on the break room wall, constant reminders that THE BEST SAFETY DEVICE IS A CAREFUL WORKER and FINGERS TAKE A LIFETIME TO GROW.) There was Dar-Dar, whose dream was to become an auto mechanic and who gave me daily updates on the ups and downs of his courtship of a red-haired girl from Cadillac. There was Fat Bill, who everyone was sure was stealing gasoline from the pump in the yard; Skinny Eddie, who took an old Chrysler off my hands for forty-nine dollars; and the Addict, the Cripple, the Preacher, and the Animal. Of these fellow dust dwellers, I remember the Animal best.

He was a wild-haired, splay-bearded man who drove a pickup with so many rust spots it looked like it was scarred with smallpox. Sometimes we would pass him on the road after work, his pickup—wreckage that belonged in the junk heap—parked on the shoulder broken down. Once we stopped and gave him a lift back to town, but all the other times, numbering about four I think, we kept going. No one at the mill spoke to the Animal much, although one day he approached me and we had a little talk about the weather. Another day he told me his wife was sickly, and he wondered, with several small mouths to feed, how he'd ever make ends meet. Up close I could see that his tangled hair was clean and his skin was spotted not with filth, as was assumed, but with the signs of premature age. In the last conversation I remember having with him, he talked rather poignantly of his parents, both of whom had recently died.

"You don't think you'll miss them, but you do," he said.

He also told me that he understood why we hadn't stopped those times he was stranded on the roadside, using the same gentle tone of voice you would use to comfort a child whose goldfish had just died. I was glad he understood because I wasn't sure I understood myself. This was the one we called an animal talking, the one we dismissed because he looked like he'd just crawled from a bog, the one whose articulations now made me ache where I'd never ached before.

Even after he found another job and quit the mill, I thought of the Animal often. When news came that oil had been discovered beneath his trailer house and a monthly check for the mineral rights had eased his burden, a part of my conscience eased, too, and I thought of him less and less.

When I remember the crew, the Animal is always the one waving.

BASEBALL

AMONG THE PHOTOGRAPHS on the museum wall in
Whipple's was a shot of the local baseball team
from a century ago. The squad is decked out in dark flannel
uniforms, their collective gaze steady and happy, determined
to rip into horsehide and base paths alike. Baseball was popular during the lumbering era, and many logging firms out-
fitted and maintained a camp or a company team. A few of
us at the mill played for local softball teams, but it's unlikely
we would have been able to organize an effective baseball
club. The obstacles were just too numerous.

The biggest hurdle was that our roster would have been
chock-full of men with mobility challenges, which meant at
least a minor logjam at two key positions. Lanny Boy, because
he was big and lumbering, would have had to play first base.
The Cat, with his lankiness, was a prototypical first baseman
and, when he wasn't threatening umpires, would have gravi-
tated in that direction. Randy, who was left-handed and had
been scoopin' 'em out of the dirt since he was eight years old
in Lansing, was really born to play first base. The Rat, built
only slightly smaller than Lanny Boy, would have been a
steady first baseman or a substitute catcher.

That was the other crowded position on the depth chart. Whiskey-Tim was squatty as an acorn and nothing if not a catcher. Skinny Eddie and Blanched Duane, both thin as bale twine, would have made scrappy catchers, as would have the Animal, whose hunched, spidery posture was rounded exactly like the kneecap of a shin guard. I had a good, strong arm and in my heart believed I was a poster boy for the position of catcher, although when I played it was usually in the outfield or at second base. To this day I tell my beloved that had I been a catcher I would have been in the big leagues, and to this day she nods without so much as a glance in my direction until the moment passes.

If my count is accurate, that is four first baseman and five catchers, at least two too many at each position. Without middle infielders and outfielders and no pitchers to speak of, the franchise was in deep trouble. (No-Doubt Brian said he was a pitcher in high school and could throw a ball eighty-five miles an hour. That's quite a heater, but no doubt this was a dubious claim. No-Doubt was a nice young man, but a backup first baseman at best.)

The Good Ole Boys would have begged off playing, claiming they were too old, and nobody would have argued with them. Any excuse for their not participating in our national pastime would have been gladly accepted (although single file, if you think about it, is the way much of the game is played, and they had a penchant for it).

Bob the maintenance man, while still in playing shape, would have been the manager of the team. Bob's skill in life was to fix things, and our team would have had obvious fixing needs. Bob used to prop his foot on the base of the chipper to remove the dull blades, a stance that reminded me of a manager propping his foot on the top step of the dugout. So, if only for aesthetical reasons, Bob would have been the man in charge. (The actual manager of the mill would have avoided the game altogether, having had enough of us during working hours.)

Dave the saw filer would have been the play-by-play announcer for the local radio station, although I think the Federal Communications Commission would have quickly intervened, for such intense sarcasm would have garbled frequencies from Milwaukee to Pawtucket. "If you think they're incompetent on the diamond, folks, you should see them in the mill," Dave would have said. "They're no good with wood there, either." "The only thing that disappeared faster than No-Doubt's last pitch was his paycheck." "Lanny moved so quickly on that last play you'd have thought it was five o'clock." And so on.

In the end what really would have held the team back wasn't the players or the broadcaster but the lack of competition. As far as I could tell, the other half of the county was all first basemen and catchers, too.

THE SAWYER

AT THE TIME I wasn't sure what to think. I suppose I was too busy pushing life's general fuss through my own emotional gristle to give it much thought. All I knew was my older brother Randy went between two realms. One realm was the sawmill proper, where one step inside the gate his position in the world changed entirely from what it was outside. Somehow inside that sawmill fence his work as a sawyer, as surely as oak trees drop acorns, transported him to a status almost Olympian. All those years, up in his booth at the south end of the mill, he manipulated levers, buttons, and, in a way, his destiny as if it were Mount Olympus itself.

You couldn't look at Randy and the sawmill and think it was anything but a perfect fit. He was even built like someone who belonged in a mill: tall, lean, square shouldered, his angles as sharp as carbon-tipped blades. With his three-day beard and thick mustache, he might have been one of those jacks in the old Moorestown photograph, staring stolidly yet gleamy-eyed into the camera.

Out of the photograph and walking, he moved somewhat stiff-legged, his eyes casting weary contemplation toward the ground a step ahead of his gait. In the cold months he wore blue jeans, a flannel shirt, an army surplus jacket, and a green stocking cap with a tiny ball on top he'd cherished since childhood. In warmer weather he dressed only somewhat lighter; the flannel shirt was replaced with a T-shirt, the stocking cap with a baseball cap.

And he smoked, three and a half packs a day, so many cigarettes they seemed as much a part of his features as a mole or dimple. With one stuck in his mouth, he resembled the Marlboro Man, although I think of his countenance as something closer to the way the old-timers described Joe DiMaggio's: mysterious and unapproachable with something inside held back. He had an inside-the-fence aura, friendly enough, but his smile was never more than pursed, a solid oak door that said No Admittance. Or maybe it said Authorized Personnel Only.

I'd find him in different towns in the years after we left the sawmill. Usually it was Houghton Lake, but there was also Merritt, Falmouth, Butterfield, Six Lakes, and Gladwin. At the end it was in whatever small town to which the small department store chain his second wife worked for had led them. Randy was no longer a sawyer, but he still worked with wood. He built grandfather clocks and gun cases. They were better than the kind you could buy in a store; they had the look of work done by a craftsman rather than an assembly line of people putting in their time.

Anyway, the setting would change, but the content of the talk never did, and now, as I recall it, the immediate settings were hardly different either. We would sit at the dining room table, Randy would have his beer and cigarettes before him, and the air would be stale with tobacco. First, we'd start in talking about the weather or the headlines or the prospects for the Detroit Tigers, warm-up talk for the main topic, which, of course, was the sawmill. When the topic was the mill, I'd do virtually all the talking; it was expected. I'd talk about Whiskey-Tim and Lanny Boy, and he'd mention that even Lanny Boy had eventually gotten fed up with the mill and left. He told me that the gang saw and the nailing machine were pulled out and hauled to a mill downstate, which meant that Henry, Gus, Del, and the Rat had lost their jobs. Sometimes he'd deliver startling news, but more often it was just shavings, odds and ends of gossip. Then he'd defer to me.

As I talked, he would slowly nod his head, his rich brown eyes staring off into the middle distance as if he weren't listening. But when I'd pause, when I'd halt the stream of reminiscences pouring off my tongue, he would ask a question or say just enough of something to get me started again. At times it felt like I was just droning on to fill the air with something other than silence, to fill it with something more than just the sound of the toke on his cigarette or the sipping noise when he tilted his glass of beer. But I'd go on anyway.

I never really tired of it. He seemed to need it, and I seemed to need his needing it, so it worked out fine. Then I'd talk about the epiphany I'd had at Moorestown while looking at the photographs on the wall at Whipple's. I didn't use the term *epiphany* then. I was excited to talk about it, but I never got grandiose. I wanted to be careful. There was a line to walk. I wanted to point out that the mill years were ones we

could be proud of without making them sound like the pin-
nacle of worldly experience. But we had been part of it: the
great Michigan lumbering tradition. It was something Michigan was known for. I would not have denied that the negative
side was tarnished gold, but there was a shiny side, too, the
14-karat side, the side that had produced a lot of good. I
wanted to point out that to be a part of it was something special for those who didn't have a military tradition or a family
business or even a clear goal in life. It was something special
for me and for him. If nothing else it was the kindling for a
conversation. Afterward, on many occasions, we built it up
to a big, hot bonfire of conversation and then left it smolder-
ing to go on to other topics. But we always came back to it to
check on it, to stoke it.

Sometimes when I'd feel myself overselling the impor-
tance of the tradition, I'd switch quickly back to the silly
stuff. To stories of me keeping watch while Lanny Boy lay on
the break room floor wiggling a screwdriver up the dispenser
of the Coke machine until a can came clattering down ("You
gotta have the touch," he would say), to me scratching "Help,
I'm being held against my will" on the side of a pallet with a
nail. He'd laugh when I told him how my spine seemed to re-
align itself whenever I heard a pulp truck gearing down on
the highway, laugh still more when I told him the constant
motion of performing the technique had often left me with a
sensation of swaying, like big oak leaves in a breeze, and that
the swaying would follow me home and pursue me through
supper, into bed, and into my dreams. I would tell him how
stacking the wood would tire me to the point of falling
asleep in the outfield during our Monday night softball

games. He seemed to want the sillier humor; he seemed to find comfort in it.

Inside the fence everyone respected him. They came from four counties, some twenty-five men, to cut, trim, and shape the wood, as men from the woods of northern Michigan—the addled, the upright, the hardy, the gentle, the repressed, and the dispossessed—had been doing for a century. They all respected Randy. It was a wide swath of people to get to take notice, much less impress, but Randy had done it unaware. The older men of the crew respected him because he worked hard and showed a genuine respect for the work itself. They saw what he was not—a truce breaker—for older workers are wary of truce breakers. Older men, weary of the world's various assortments of grief, both mental and physical, and their part in it, look on work as the truce established with such a world. The foundation of the truce, the peace they've made with the world, is this deal: I'll do this undesirable work, and, largely, I'll be left alone.

In Randy they saw a young man who understood this. They respected him because he ran a complex piece of machinery, made good money, and kept his mouth closed, although they certainly listened when he opened it. The younger workers respected him because he managed all of this without becoming a company man.

And, the sawyer's pride, his cut was true. Had, say, Hemingway cast the long eye to a cant or board Randy had cut, he would have said it was good and true and lovely. He would have recognized the talent; he might even have recognized a gift. Randy had it, especially with wood. Wood was his thing and always had been.

He could swing a baseball bat, which in those years in the youth leagues of Lansing was made of wood, like the young DiMaggio himself. With his jackknife he whittled sticks into arrows and with perfect technique notched longer, thicker sticks to make bows. He carved race cars out of blocks of pine for the Pine Wood Derby in the Cub Scouts and in shop class sculpted a gouge dish, wooden ducks, and a cribbage board from chunks of mahogany. With tools and scrap wood scattered around him, he built a wall in our house in Lansing so our sister could have a room of her own, in the process explaining to me what a level, cross stud, and miter box are (and shaking his head at my ignorance). He took the building trades class in high school and made the sports page of the *Lansing State Journal* his senior year, a large photograph of him putting the finishing touches on the dugout the trades class had built at a local baseball field. The day would come when he would build his own house from a floor plan he'd drawn up on a legal pad. Shaping wood was his game. Inside the sawmill fence he had found his niche.

And he was steady. He lopped boards, cants, and railroad ties from the logs as if he were using a big carrot peeler rather than the rickety and more ancient of the two head saws in the mill, the wood coming down the chain symmetrical, slippery, and ready to be stacked.

It had taken him nine months to get comfortable with the saw, an astounding pace for a perfectionist. Operating a head saw required timing, precision, and a level head; it required the ability to get a feel for things in a hurry and an eye as sharp as a leadoff man's. These were qualities Randy had in abundance, but outside the fence, during those months, I remember he worried about being good enough. I was off on one of my college stints then, but I knew enough about saw-mills to know that sawyering was an important job fraught with responsibility and everything that happened in the mill revolved around it. Randy bore through the doubts, fretted, learned, fretted some more, and then one day realized he'd become nothing short of a sawyer extraordinaire. Out of the minors and into the majors. A power hitter. Master of the true cut. He was only twenty-one years old.

One night there it was on the local evening news: the saw-mill, burning down. There were several fire trucks in the mill yard, and long hoses stretched across the ground like copper-skinned snakes. A fireman was speaking into the camera about how significant the heat had been, how it had twisted metal. It was believed the fire had begun in an electrical box, and arson was not suspected. The segment had been introduced by the newsperson saying that the mill had been one of the county's largest employers. A dozen years had passed since I'd worked at the mill, but I could easily recall my wish that it would burn down. If the mill would only burn down, I used to think, I could lie around and draw unemployment benefits for a few weeks before anyone could work up a good complaint against my slothfulness. But I felt bad watching those flames on TV. Mill hands were out of work, a business thwarted, a sawmill gone. Fire. The fate of sawmills. I called Randy to hear if he had heard, and he had. He laughed politely when I said, "Now it burns down." He seemed preoccupied.

I remember something that happened when we were boys. I was eleven or twelve, Randy around fourteen. Our older brother, Skeeter, had come down with the flu, so Randy and I stood in on his paper route. The *Lansing State Journal* was dropped off in three bundles at the edge of our yard in our blue-collar neighborhood just north of the city limits. We added inserts to the papers, loaded them into the big canvas bags, and started off through the cold spring afternoon. We delivered up one side of Hannah Street, down the other, back and forth along Hazel, then up Florence and along Pearl, streets named for the great-aunts of one of our neighbors.

Delivering a newspaper to a customer's house, like stacking a cant, required a brisk technique of its own. First you opened the screen door and held the paper at waist level against the inner door, then, pulling your hand back, you dropped the paper as you whisked the screen door closed again. Open, drop, slam. The idea was for the customer to open his or her door and have the paper flop into the living room or entryway with the headlines showing.

After Pearl, you crossed U.S. 27 and made a couple of deliveries on State Road with jogs up Brooks and Northward. Then it was on to Eskes Street. Eskes made the paper route interesting. We never called it Eskes Street; we called it Dog Avenue. All up and down this infamous stretch of asphalt were dogs: big ones, small ones, barkers, chasers, and nippers with names like Gretchen, Scottie, Bebe, and Rufus.

Of all the dogs only one would actually bite. We didn't know his name. He was tied behind a house at the mouth of the street, a stout mixed breed, mostly beagle, but with several pounds of rottweiler. The good news was his owners didn't take a paper. The bad news was it didn't matter, for this pooch was willing to cross borders to plunder.

As we turned onto Dog Avenue, I said to Randy, "What if he's loose?"

Randy's stoic expression never changed. "He's never loose."

I was nervous. I never took the calm, calculating approach to anything. Mean dogs were to be feared first, dealt with second. The emotional response first, always. For Randy, the dog was just something to be dealt with.

"But what if he is?" I asked.

Randy looked straight ahead. "Then I'll take care of him."

We walked up Eskes, delivering along the west side, crossed over and delivered midway down the east side, and then crossed back. You had to make this last crossing to get the correct angle on the backyard of the house where the hound lived. At first glance I didn't see him back there.

"Maybe they got rid . . . ," I began, but Randy was shaking his head.

"Here he comes," he said. He was calmer than oatmeal in a bowl.

Sure enough the dog had spotted his prey and was barreling along the near side of the house, across the yard, toward us. He was thirty yards away . . . twenty . . . I could that see his tail wasn't wagging. That's how you knew if they were mean, the stillness of that tail. This one meant business.

Randy's voice never changed. "Stay calm. Don't move."

He might have been helping you with a math problem, telling you not to forget your decimal point or carry your three. The dog was at full gallop, five yards away, when Randy began to swing his paper bag. With a *whoosh* the dog's head was suddenly covered in canvas. He stumbled, got up, and

Randy whopped him again. I threw a pop bottle at him, which glanced off a broad flank and careened across the road. The dog backed out of Randy's bag, gave us a blank stare, and turned and hauled for home.

Randy smiled intrepidly as we watched him go. "Always go for the head," he said. "That's the only thing they understand."

It was marvelous. The whole time I had not felt the least doubt of victory. It seemed the sky, the road, the scant grass, everything, were accomplices in the plan that the dog would do us no harm. And Randy was at the center of it somehow, his small realm, for that moment, on Dog Avenue. It was the same way at the mill. And when he moved the center of the realm shifted with him.

It was in Stratford. Not Stratford-upon-Avon, not Stratford, Ontario, but Stratford, Michigan, a lumber town in northern Missaukee County. Population zero unless you counted the ghosts. When the ghosts weren't ghosts, the population was a few hundred, maybe a thousand.

I arrived there by driving north out of Moorestown, following the road on a wide bend to the east and another back to the north until a sunlit meadow appeared on the right, a little notch in the eastern edge of the Dead Stream Swamp. I pulled into a small grassy lot stumped off for parking. The ruins of Stratford lay adjacent.

There were a few trees and a two-track winding back into the swamp; otherwise the ruins were hardly more than a vacant lot. Wooden signs, the smaller ones shaped like arrows, pointed out where buildings and railroad tracks once sat.

One sign read WYE TRACK, another DEPOT. A sign leaning against a crabapple tree read RAPID CITY 32 MILES. The largest sign, near the road, gave a concise history of the site.

SITE OF THE
VILLAGE OF STRATFORD

> This town originated in 1897 with the purchase
> of 13,400 acres of virgin red and white pine by
> The Thayer Lumber Company. A railroad came
> the same year and hauled logs six days per
> week for twelve years. In 1908 the last of the
> pine logs were hauled and Stratford became
> deserted. The site was purchased by the
> state in 1937.

CONSERVATION DEPARTMENT

Now, over a century later, not a sliver of scrap wood, not a foundation stone (if ever one existed) remained. Stratford was a marbleless Athens. But the air—it seemed as green as the foliage—and the silence nudged my imagination awake. Stratford, I was sure, existed for the sake of imagination and memory.

As I waded through the tall grass and ferns, I could imagine the small houses of timber, could actually see the small impressions in the ground where outhouses once sat. As I went on, the two-track, used by berry pickers, bird-watchers, and dirt bikers, suddenly metamorphosed into a grade with ties and rails, the engine of a semitruck gearing down on Route 55 twelve miles to the south became a kind of whistle, and a train, the 119 from Rapid City, rolled through my fantasy and into Stratford.

I imagined this with the clarity of a well-conditioned film from, say, 1959, a film shot in color although grayer shades prevailed. At first it seemed there was no one on the train, but then, ducking out of the passenger car and descending the narrow passage of steel steps, the conductor venerably lit on the platform. He stood beside me, and the Stratford we gazed on wasn't the ruins of 1997 but the thriving place of 1897, complete with homes, store, livery, and, of course, a sawmill. In fact I imagined a huddle of men just coming off their shift at the mill, walking through a big slatted door toward us, pale and ghostly at first but becoming more recognizable the closer they came. The conductor smiled at my expression of recognition as I watched Whiskey-Tim, Lanny Boy, the Cat, the Rat, and the others advance through time with the certainty of the smile advancing across my face.

"We rode the train," I say. "We were part of history," and I mean History, the real thing, the kind remembered, the kind even cobbled into the corner of a textbook and a memoir or two. The conductor says, "Well, yes," and he is still smiling. It's then that I realize he moves stiff-legged, is angular, and is as quiet as a pot of warm soup. And it's then that I realize he's the one who has ushered me onto the train at least twice (for I had worked in two sawmills), that he is more than just the conductor, that imagination and memory have fused. That he so resembles Randy has something to do with my aching wish to have even five more minutes with my deceased brother. He died at the age of forty, pulled down and drowned by a despair I was never able to penetrate, although

if I had another chance I would find a way not to fail him. . . .
Just five more minutes, I think, as the scene fades. . . . Five
minutes. . . . What would I give for that?

One step outside the fence and everything changed. In the
civilian world the metaphysics went haywire. Mount Olympus sank below sea level. With the exception of his young
daughters and for the most part his wife, no one seemed to
see any semblance of the man inside the fence. At the time,
with a bird's-eye view into both realms, I didn't know what to
think. Or maybe, as I've said, I didn't think about it enough.
All I knew was that the difference between one place and the
other was evident because outside the fence he drank.

It was beer. A ton of it. It took the edge off and made him
easy. He was quiet, stoic, to begin with, and the beer made
him smiley, friendly, a little sloppy. Every night after work we
would drive to the Trading Post Party Store and Randy
would buy a six-pack. On Friday nights it was a twelve-pack.
I abstained during the week, but on weekends I drank with
him. Sometimes we would pop the first top at noon, sometimes two, sometimes as late as eight o'clock. We'd drink
until one or two o'clock in the morning, watch the ballgame
on TV, play catch with a softball, eat pizza. The girls would
come into the yard, and we would play Wiffle ball with
them, beautiful little girls in dresses with watermelon prints.
Sometimes we would climb into the truck and travel the
back roads around Merritt, drinking and gossiping. Most of
the time, though, we sat on the couch and talked about the
mill. We talked about the mill a lot. Sometimes with humor,
sometimes raw with complaint, and always, as the empties

piled up, with a touch of resignation. A life could have passed this way and no one would have thought much about it.

But he drank at weddings, reunions, Sunday dinners, and picnics. He drank until he was sleepy, and then he'd get up, take a beer in hand, stuff another in his hip pocket, and go. A beer in your hip pocket is a problem. This was when people began to give him the eye. And the eye, after a while, whether he was drunk or not, is what he got from people.

The eye is wariness itself. It's the wonder over just how hard someone's edges will bake. The eye is avoidance; to give someone the eye is to give up on them or the beginnings of giving up. The eye is what Randy got instead of conversation. This was a disaster because a stoic man needs conversation even if his part in it is only to grunt, occasionally nod, or smile. A silent, brooding man will rely on others to chatter because chatter creates an atmosphere, a realm to be at home in, safe in. Chatter, or idle conversation, is like blowing feathers into a burlap sack. It might be a useless activity, but on the other hand it might result in the most comfortable pillow you've ever laid your head on. But with the eye the notion of comfort is strangled. With the eye you get silence or, at best, murmurs. And once the wary eye opens, it's difficult to make it close again.

When was it I stopped chattering? I don't recall exactly. Maybe a year or so into my time at the mill. All I know is that there were many nights of hauling Randy out of the truck, his six-foot-plus frame over my shoulder, and carrying him into the house. Dead, loose weight; there was no technique for it. You did the best you could, fought off the guilt as best you could, because you had just been out half the night with a guy who had a problem. You were drunk, too, but not to the point of oblivion. The previous sentence is not meant to blunt the excess of my own behavior but to point out that there was a difference. With the drinking came the borrowing of money and a kind of sullenness that sought to pull me into his misery—and here another old adage applies—not in any harmful way but *just for the company.* Finally, I could feel the eye developing in myself.

When was he going to get a hold on things? When was he going to see that the phase was over or should be over? At some point you realize that he might never see it and it might never be over. And it's a terrible thing inside you to know that as close as you were—brothers, friends—you felt the impulse to give up on him, too. To know that the bond was pulled so thin that it had upset the footing between you. To know that your empathy had also begun to fray into avoidance. It's a bad feeling, the developing eye, because next comes resignation, and then it becomes too late to see objects of the eye in any different light. The sight of them makes a noise in your head; they creak like barbed wire in the wind.

But one morning in May the grader showed up and I was drawn back from the brink of resignation concerning Randy. A few seconds, a quick exchange, drew me back. It was the most unexpected thing that happened to me at the sawmill. I was sure I was gone, that I'd never lose the eye, and the truth is I never lost the eye completely. But to give Randy the eye was never again my first impulse. My first impulse, though I failed too often to follow it, was to never give up on him.

That morning I had been assigned to throw for the grader, the task most dreaded among stackers. This belligerent assignment kept you awake the night before, staring wide-eyed at the ceiling, the blanket pulled to your chin, your toes twittering, wondering why you hadn't taken a job in a gas station.

The grader was hired to do just that: grade oak boards for scale and quality, boards that would be sold to the furniture companies downstate. The grader stood atop the pile, his scaling stick and notebook in hand, grading the boards one by one, calling out left or right so the thrower would know in which pile to toss the boards. The grader worked fast, and when he called left or right he meant his left or right, so as thrower you had to think to toss the board opposite his call. Throwing and thinking did nothing together except create a boiling frustration.

It was a cold morning, but five minutes into the job I'd already slung my jacket aside and could feel streams of sweat tickling my rib cage. The grader, a man of around thirty, was pleasant enough, but he seemed slightly put out to have to pause so I could keep my two piles tidy. In the meantime I bent, grabbed, and flung as fast as I could, my lungs and joints burning with equal fury. Left, right, left, right, when it was really right, left, right, left, everything counter to what you expected, your life a scale of dwindling hope, of dreams rent, a life of such smothered barometer you actually wished to be bagging groceries or changing oil instead. But no sir, you had been talked out of those jobs.

At ten o'clock that morning, having glimpsed Randy's lean figure come past the chip van, I dropped the board I was holding, groused to the grader that it was break time, snatched my jacket off the ground, and strode angrily for the gate. The springtime sun threw a slant of yellow light across my chest, but my heart didn't warm.

I reached the truck first, and when Randy climbed in the symphony, or maybe it was the litany, of complaint for having been misled, snickered, hoodwinked, and various other inscrutables and inaccountables gushed off my tongue. Randy sat calmly, staring first through the window and then down into his Thermos cup, listening as he was blamed, in tone if not actual word, for every regret and misfortune that had ever beset his plank-stacking brother. Finally he pointed across the road and asked, "What do you notice?"

"About what?" I asked heatedly.

"Right in front of us."

I looked but didn't get it. The hood of the truck? The mill? What was he talking about?

"The gate," Randy said.

"What about it?" I snapped.

"It's always open."

In other words, he was telling me, don't let it hit you in the hind end on the way out. He was fed up. I was a spectacle, a whiner and a pitiful one at that. He said none of this, but then there was no need to say it. His rock solid message had plummeted to the bottom of my shallow puddle with a thud. It was a message difficult to swallow. It was like a quick punch in the nose that brings tears to your eyes. You wanted to deny it, in large part because it came from someone with a drinking problem, a guy people had stopped believing in, a young man who had stopped believing in himself. But the message he delivered was irrefutable. It was time to stop being so angry. I was angry about many things at once, mostly with myself for being young and not too smart and having made mistakes.

But I could fix most of these mistakes. Certainly I could. It was time to listen to Randy. It was time to listen because he was doing more than just telling me that the gate was open. He was letting me go. He had just released his grip as softly as he possibly could. I don't think he wanted to. But he loved me. And I, in the singular way brothers do, loved him. Sometimes barbed wire creaks sweetly in the wind.

At that moment I decided I would go back to college. It was the right thing, and whatever doubts I had about the route in that direction had just been cleared by my brother's true and lovely cut.

Randy sipped his coffee one more time and flung the grounds out the window. He screwed the top back on the Thermos, and we sat quietly until the break was over. Then we got out of the truck and walked back across Bacon Street to the sawmill, together, as we had somewhere near a thousand times before.

That August I left the sawmill. On my last day Lanny Boy came up and shook my hand and said it had been good to work with me. Red Eye bid me good luck, and Skinny Eddie said so long. For just a sprig of a second, I felt a pull in my tear ducts, but Randy stood nearby and would have never let me forget it had I cried. So I blinked away the notion, blinked it away for a dozen years. Then I stood in the dry yard looking across the furrows and the ruts toward the mill with its big open door, dark as always, and the place seemed to be less a freighter, as it had on my first day, than a big cartoon caboose, yawning. But the moment really wasn't comical. Big Tom came up, shook my hand, and bid me good luck with an expression so solemn it was as if he hadn't quite known how to approach me. I thought back to the day a few months earlier when I'd wanted so badly to be through the gate and home and realized there had been no hurry after all. I knew then that I'd swallowed it all wrong somehow, that my guard had been up too high and I had not realized it was a mighty enough guard to block out experience.

The manager never did say good-bye. At quitting time on that last day, he busied himself with something in the yard and never bothered to shake my hand or even glance my way. I was angry over that and vowed I would never return to the mill to work or even visit. Of course that was silly. I have been back infinitely.

ONCE MORE TO THE MILL

A FEW NIGHTS EACH MONTH I wander down to help out in the tiny sawmill my neighbor has rigged in the north end of his cattle barn. An old hand lending a hand is how I think of it. I'll stack cants and toss boards, and occasionally I'll climb aboard his ancient forklift to move a heap of slabwood from one dusty spot to another. It's there—on the forklift—that I feel it, a tingling, something else I can only describe as a lifting sensation, and a shaking out. I'm not sure what all this is, but it feels a lot like redemption.

Redemption because thirty years ago at the sawmill I refused to learn how to drive the forklift. The crux of my argument against mixing lumber stacking with forklift driving was that before you knew it you would be jamming two jobs into one skin yet the little blue envelope wouldn't hold any taller numbers come payday.

I remember the look on the foreman's face as I explained this. A predecessor of Big Tom, his name was Walt, a handsome dish-faced man whose expression of surprise and pity hangs in my memory like a sullen moon. When you're forty-five, Walt's look seemed to say, such a stand could be called a bargaining position. But when you're twenty it's just plain stubbornness.

For years my chief regret was that I hadn't taken a broader view of the thing, that I hadn't viewed the forklift as a chance to improve myself, to gain a skill I might use in the future, that I—and this is the heart, the throbbing ventricles of the regret—had bypassed the adventure of it. If you think forklift driving is decidedly unadventurous, consider that I'm one of those unmechanical souls who needs directions to work a drinking fountain and you'll get the idea.

But then all that changed. One burnished afternoon, passing by my neighbor's barn, I invited myself in to have a gander at his operation and stacked a few cants for nothing. My neighbor, who's no fool, said I could come back anytime. I kneaded driving the forklift into our tacit bargain, and after some initial herky-jerkyness—a bit of spilled maple and a little gear grinding—I sit atop this wonderful machine not knowing whether to gloat or float.

And it's funny about the forklift. An anecdote from my day job will hardly spawn a rustle in the listener, but a forklift offering is, well, something else. There are two basic reactions. Some listeners go bright in the eyes, their ears expand a good six inches, and they pine for every detail, from the make of the machine to how often I drive it, from the location of the mill to what kind of wood we cut. For these folks you can see that forklift talk is the chocolate in their cauliflower day, and they are humored into what I call the enthusiastic reaction. The other is the gloomy reaction. This occurs when the listeners squint and cock their heads, their confoundedness clicking louder than horseshoes on concrete in the cover of their envy. They're thinking you can explain landing a rocket ship on Mars (science), you can explain a daft man becoming rich (luck in the lottery), but Randy's brother driving a forklift? What's going on here? Their faces pucker with that "why do you get to do the exquisite thing and I don't" wince or, if they're the Rookie's wife, the "why do you get to do the exquisite thing and my husband doesn't" wince, and they fall to listening in blustery silence. They figure there's no explanation for it other than that a chunk of luck traveling for eons through interstellar space finally dropped out of the sky and clunked me on the head.

I think they might be right. Of course, once I get the gloomy reaction, I pour it on. I lift an eyebrow and lower the boom as it were. I tell them about the forklift brakes, which don't work, that the only thing you get pressing the brake pedal is a little exercise for your ankle. Hearing this is like hearing that I have gone from shooting rats in the dump with a .22 to killing rattlesnakes in the garden with a ruler. Knowing they can't top that, their gloom turns from a roadside mist to a swampland fog. Why is redemption all the sweeter knowing I could drive through the barn wall if I'm not careful?

But for a stack of reasons I don't rub it in too hard. For one thing, I'd like to keep the snakes in the analogical realm. Another is that I'm a novice forklift driver at best. Third, and this is the big one, I know I'm lucky to have worked in an industry with a tradition of attracting the eccentric and rambunctious and in which twenty months of labor put a steaming pot of stories on the stove, the lid always quivering to let one out. Not everyone has been so fortunate.

Does this explain the strange impulse of wanting to drive a thirdhand forklift? I don't know. Sometimes even while doing it I wonder why I'm doing it. But then, through the big barn door, I'll catch a glimpse of the big pine tree across the road and the Big Dipper above it, a stunner of a sight not to be had at any other angle. Then there are those nights when the sawdust, moistened by a late autumn rain and nudged by a gentle wind, seems to be a ribbon of glitter in the air, a veritable banner of purist motives, and the stars before my eyes. It makes me think of Randy, who is at peace now, of Lanny Boy and Whiskey-Tim and all the rest, and it's then I know that driving the forklift will never turn memories into living flesh but it is one less thing to mourn.